ADAM HAMILTON'S

The Journey

Walking the Road to Bethlehem

Children's Edition

Daphna Flegal

Abingdon Press
Nashville

The Journey
Walking the Road to Bethlehem
Children's Edition

Production Editor: Julie P. Glass
Designer: Mark Foltz
Art—pp. 4, 14–18, 28, 41, 54: Megan Jeffery; pp. 11, 29, 40, 52, 61: Robert S. Jones

Daphna Flegal lives in Nashville, Tennessee, where she is a writer and editor of children's curriculum resources. She is a diaconal minister in the West Michigan conference of The United Methodist Church, where she served in local congregations as Director of Children's Ministries and Director of Christian Education. She presently serves as lead editor for children's resources at The United Methodist Publishing House. She is most excited about her newest job— grandmother!

PACP00914605-01

ISBN 978-1-426-72857-0

11 12 13 14 15 16 17 18 19 20—10 9 8 7 6 5 4 3 2 1

Printed in the U. S. A.

CONTENTS

Your church can do a churchwide study of *The Journey: Walking the Road to Bethlehem* by using the children's resource, *The Journey: Walking the Road to Bethlehem Children's Edition* by Daphna Flegal; the youth resource, *The Journey: Youth Edition* by Jason Gant; and the adult resource, *The Journey: Walking the Road to Bethlehem* by Adam Hamilton.

Art Show

You are invited to an art show

in celebration of the birth of Jesus.

The art show will be in

_____.

at _____.

Please bring a new baby blanket as your ticket into the show.

Suggestions for an All-Church Event

The Journey: Walking the Road to Bethlehem explores the story of Jesus' birth with fresh eyes and ears in an effort to discover the real meaning of Christmas. Author Adam Hamilton draws upon insights gained from historians, archaeologists, biblical scholars, and theologians, and from walking in the places where the story occurred.

A churchwide Advent program for all ages will help people come to a deeper understanding of what the Christmas story teaches us about Jesus Christ and about God's will for our lives. It will offer opportunities for learning, for intergenerational projects and activities, and for reaching out to the community.

Resources for the Churchwide Study

Adults
The Journey: Walking the Road to Bethlehem—Book
The Journey: A Season of Reflections—
  Devotional companion
The Journey: DVD with Leader's Guide—Videos
  (optional for youth)

Youth
The Journey: Youth Edition—Leader's Guide

Children
*The Journey: Walking the Road to Bethlehem Children's
  Edition*—Leader's Guide

Schedule

Many churches have weeknight programs that include an evening meal; an intergenerational gathering time; and classes for children, youth, and adults. The following schedule illustrates one way to organize a weeknight program.

5:30 PM	Meal
6:00 PM	Intergenerational gathering introducing Bible characters and places for the lesson. This time may include presentations, skits, music, and opening or closing prayers.
6:15 PM–8:45 PM	Classes for children, youth, and adults

Churches may want to do the Advent study as a Sunday school program. This setting would be similar to the weeknight setting. The following schedule takes into account a shorter class time. which is the norm for Sunday morning programs.

10 minutes	Intergenerational gathering
45 minutes	Classes for children, youth, and adults

Choose a schedule that works best for your congregation and its existing Christian education programs.

Activity Suggestions

All-Church Art Show

Directions for an art show can be found in each lesson of the children's study. The final art show is in Lesson 5.

All-Church Baby-Blanket Drive

Ask participants to bring new baby blankets to give to a homeless shelter, battered women's shelter, or food pantry. Let the blankets be the tickets to enter the art show.

Costumed Greeters

Recruit volunteers to dress up as the different biblical characters being studied each week. For the first lesson, recruit an adult or youth to dress as the angel Gabriel. Have Gabriel greet each person at the door with the words, "Rejoice, *(person's name)*, favored one! The Lord is with you!" There are scripts and suggestions for each lesson in the children's study.

An Amazing Race

Divide the participants into intergenerational groups to play "An Amazing Race." The directions for the game are found in Lesson 3 of the children's study.

1 Mary

Objectives
The children will
- hear Luke 1:26-38.
- discover that God chose Mary, a young girl from the small village of Nazareth, to give birth to God's Son.
- learn how Mary responded to God.
- explore ways they can respond to God.

Bible Story
Luke 1:26-38, CEB: The angel Gabriel visits Mary.

Bible Verse
Luke 1:38, CEB: Then Mary said, "I am the Lord's servant. Let it be with me just as you have said."

Focus for the Teacher

An Unlikely Choice

Mary was probably thirteen or fourteen years old when she was surprised by the angel Gabriel, a messenger from God. Even though she seems young to us, in New Testament times Mary was already considered to be an adult and was engaged to be married to Joseph. An engagement usually lasted a year and was considered as binding as marriage.

The angel Gabriel came to Mary in Nazareth, her hometown. Mary was confused and frightened by the appearance of Gabriel—who wouldn't be? But Gabriel calms Mary's fears and tells her that she will give birth to a baby boy named Jesus.

The name "Jesus" is the Greek translation for "Joshua," or in Hebrew, "Yeshua," and means "The Lord is salvation" or "God saves."

The angel continues with the news that Mary's baby will be God's Son and a great king. Mary still does not understand how this can happen. After all, she is only engaged, not married. But Gabriel reminds her that with God, all things are possible.

> Then Mary said, "I am the Lord's servant. Let it be with me just as you have said."
>
> Luke 1:38, CEB

The Bible Verse

Even though Mary might have been frightened and confused, her response was to answer God's call with a yes—"I am the Lord's servant. Let it be with me just as you have said" (Luke 1:38, CEB). This response is even more significant when we remember that Mary's pregnancy during her engagement would be considered a sign of adultery, and a woman caught in adultery could be stoned to death. Yet, Mary still responded to God's message with acceptance.

Nazareth

Nazareth was a small village three to four miles from a larger city called Sepphoris. Sepphoris was more prosperous and well known than Nazareth. The people in Sepphoris lived in luxury villas, while many people in Nazareth lived in caves or used caves as part of their homes. In fact, the people who lived in Nazareth were probably the workers and servants for the people in Sepphoris. Yet, it is a young unknown girl from the small village of Nazareth that God chose to give birth to God's Son.

Explore Interest Groups

Be sure that adult leaders are waiting when the first child arrives. Greet and welcome each child. Get the child involved in an activity that interests him or her and introduces the theme for the day's activities.

The Lord Is With You!

- Recruit an adult or teenager to dress as the angel Gabriel (with or without wings) to greet each child as he or she enters the room. This person will also tell the story as Gabriel during large-group time.

- Have each child make a nametag. Give each child a copy of the nametag (page 14); there are four nametags on the page.

- Let older children write their names on the nametags with black permanent markers. Use the permanent marker yourself and write the names for younger children.

- Lightly tape each nametag onto a rough surface. This could be a piece of corrugated cardboard, ridged shelf paper, or a brick wall or rough floor.

- Show the children how to use the side of a brown crayon (with paper removed) to rub over the nametags. You will still see the name through the rubbing.

- Show each child how to crumple the nametag into a ball and then smooth it out again. Have them repeat the crumpling and smoothing process several times.

- **Say:** We've made our nametags look like scrolls from Bible times. Today we will hear the story about the angel's visit to a young woman named Mary. When the angel came to Mary, he called her by name. Go to our angel and have him (or her) help you put on your nametag.

- Encourage each child to take his or her nametag to the person portraying Gabriel. Gabriel tapes the nametag to each child's clothing and blesses each child.

- **Gabriel says:** Rejoice, *(child's name)*, favored one! The Lord is with you!

At Home in Nazareth

- Invite the children to experience Mary's home in Nazareth.

- Set up different "home" stations. These may be as simple or as elaborate as you wish. You can simply set supplies on a table or decorate the area to be Bible-times homes.

Prepare

- ✓ Photocopy a nametag (page 14) for each child.

- ✓ Provide black permanent markers, brown crayons with papers removed, safety scissors, and masking tape.

- ✓ Recruit an adult or teenager to be Gabriel.

- ✓ Provide a white robe for Gabriel's costume.

- **Say:** Mary was a normal young woman in Bible times. She was probably thirteen or fourteen years old. It seems young to us, but in Bible times she was old enough to be engaged to a man named Joseph. Mary probably did all the things women did in Bible times, like bake bread and go to the well to get water. Let's do some of the things Mary might have done each day in Nazareth.

Bake Bread

- Set up a grinding stone in one section of this station. Place a stack of newspapers on the floor. Then place a flat rock or wooden cutting board on the newspaper. Sprinkle millet seed, barley kernels, or wheat kernels on the cutting board or flat rock.

- Show the children how to use the round rock to smash the grain onto the flat rock or cutting board.

- **Say:** Every morning the women in the family began making bread by grinding grain. The grain was crushed between stones in small, hand-operated mills to make flour.

- Have the children wash their hands.

- Give each child a piece of wax paper and a biscuit.

- Have the children dust their hands with flour.

- Show the children how to knead their biscuits on the wax paper and then flatten them into thin round disks.

- **Say:** Next, the women added water and yeast to the flour to make dough. The women kneaded the dough for about one hour. Then they made the dough into thin, flat loaves that were about the size of a dinner plate. The thin loaves were put on a round piece of clay and baked in the oven. The oven was outside near the doorway of the house or in the courtyard.

- Place the flattened biscuits on a baking sheet. Bake the biscuits according to the directions on the package. Plan to serve the biscuits during small-group time.

Mary's Well

- Encourage the children to help you set up a well in your large-group area.

- Place a large plastic tablecloth or drop cloth on the floor. Place a large plastic or metal tub in the center of the cloth.

- Let the children make paper-bag stones to set around the tub to build the well.

- Have the children stuff crumpled newspaper into the bags.

- Fold over the top of the bags and secure with tape.

- Show the children how to stack the pretend stones around the well.

Prepare

✓ Provide recycled newspapers; flat rock or wooden cutting board; round rock; millet seed, barley kernels, or wheat kernels; biscuit dough; flour; wax paper; baking sheets; oven; and hand-washing supplies.

✓ Preheat oven according to directions on the biscuits.

Prepare

✓ Provide a large plastic tablecloth or drop cloth, brown paper bags, recycled newspapers, masking tape, plastic or metal tub, two plastic buckets, rope, water, and towels.

- **Say:** The village of Nazareth had a well with a spring as its source of water. At this spring, the water came up to the surface of the ground. People in Nazareth walked to the well to get the water they would need each day. Women often gathered at the well or spring to talk to each other about what was happening in the village. Mary would have gone to the well in Nazareth.

- Pour water into the tub inside your well. Tie a rope onto a plastic bucket and set it beside the well. Place another plastic bucket nearby.

- Let each child take a turn holding the rope and lowering the bucket into the tub to get water in the bucket. Encourage the child to pull up the bucket and then pour the water into the second bucket.

- Pour the water back into the well for the next child's turn.

Walk to the Well

- **Say:** Women in Bible times often carried the large clay jars filled with water from the well on their heads.

- Line the children up on the opposite side of the room from the "well."

- Give the first child in line a plastic cup. Have the child place the cup on his or her head and walk across the room to the well. If the cup falls, the child must give the cup to next child in line and then move to the back of the line. The new cupbearer now tries to walk to the well.

- Add a small amount of water to the cup, if having water will work in your setting. Have towels available to wipe up spills.

Prepare

✓ Provide plastic cups, optional: water and towels.

Great Artists at Work

- **Say:** Many artists have painted pictures of Mary. One artist is Botticelli. Botticelli lived in the 1400s. He painted a beautiful picture of Mary called the *Madonna of the Magnificat. Madonna* is another name many people call Mary. *Magnificat* is the name we give the song Mary sang to praise God for her baby.

- Show the children the *Madonna of the Magnificat.*

- **Say:** Look at the people in this painting. They are the wife and children of the man who paid Botticelli for the painting. The man's wife is Mary and his children are the young men and women. Today you will be the great artists. Paint a picture of Mary. You may draw yourself or someone you know as Mary. You may draw other people you know, maybe a brother or a sister, your mother or father, in the picture around Mary.

- Give each child a piece of paper. Let older children trace a large paper plate onto the paper. Have the children cut out the circles. Precut the circles for younger children.

- Encourage the children to use pencils to sketch their pictures of Mary. Let the children add color to their pictures with paint or colored pencils.

- Save the paintings for an art show in Lesson 5.

Prepare

✓ Provide paper plates, newspapers or plastic tablecloth, large drawing paper, pencils, paint smocks, washable paints and brushes or colored pencils.

✓ Cover the table with newspapers or a plastic tablecloth. If you use paint, have the children wear smocks.

✓ Cut circles for younger children.

✓ Provide a copy of the *Madonna of the Magnificat* by Botticelli. Search online or in the library for images of the painting.

Large Group

Bring all the children together to experience the Bible story. Use jingle bells to alert the children to the large-group time.

Servant Sweep

- **Say:** Many homes in Nazareth were built into caves. Caves were cool in the summer and warm in the winter. Other homes were built with rocks or mud bricks. The floor was often made of packed dirt. Women were usually responsible for sweeping the dirt floor. Mary probably helped sweep the floor at her home.

- Have the children line up in teams on one side of the room. Place a basket on the other side of the room opposite each team. Place the rolled-up Bible verse squares in the baskets.

- Give the first person in each line a whisk broom. When you say "Go!," have the child hold the whisk broom and hop across the floor to the basket. Then the child draws a Bible verse roll from the basket, places it on the floor, and uses the whisk broom to sweep the roll back to the line.

- Have the first sweeper keep the Bible verse roll, but give the broom to the next child in line.

- When the last person on the team returns to the line with the broom, have everyone on the team open their Bible rolls and then shout Mary's words printed on the rolls, "I am the Lord's servant" (Luke 1:38, CEB).

Prepare

✓ Provide a whisk broom and a basket for each team.

✓ Photocopy and cut apart the Bible verse (page 15, top). You will need one square for each child.

✓ Roll each square into a tube and tape the ends together.

✓ Place the Bible verse rolls into the baskets. Place a basket opposite each team.

Now Appearing at Nazareth

- Recruit an adult or teenager to portray Gabriel. Give the actor a photocopy of the script (page 19) and provide a costume.

- Have the children sit down in front of the well (see page 8).

- **Say:** Listen to today's Bible story.

- Begin reading Luke 1:26-38 from a CEB Bible. Have Gabriel interrupt you right after verse 28 by swooping in among the children and shouting his first lines. Stop reading and leave the stage area to Gabriel.

Prepare

✓ Recruit an adult or teenager to portray Gabriel.

✓ Photocopy the script (page 19) for the actor.

✓ Provide a CEB Bible and an angel costume (with or without wings).

✓ Use the well made earlier (page 8).

Walking to Nazareth

- Divide the children into groups of no more than eight.

- Give each child a pencil or crayon and a copy of the Nazareth map (page 15). Point out the name *Nazareth*. Spell the name for the children.

- Play Christmas music from a CD or sing a Christmas carol. As the music plays, let the children walk around the circle.

- Stop the music and have the children stop walking.

Prepare

✓ Provide a Christmas music CD, a CD player, pencils or crayons, marker, scissors, and construction paper.

- Instruct each child to look at the letter she or he is standing on. Have the child use the pencil or crayon to circle the matching letter on the Nazareth map. Help younger children as needed.

- Play the music and have the children walk around the circle again.

- Continue playing the game until all the children have circled every letter on their maps.

Bible Verse Hot Potato

- Have the children stand in their circle groups.

- Repeat the Bible verse with the children several times: "Then Mary said, 'I am the Lord's servant. Let it be with me just as you have said'" (Luke 1:38, CEB).

- Pass a ball around the circle (like Hot Potato) as the children speak each word of the Scripture in unison. When the children get to the word "servant," whoever is holding the ball must call out, "Luke 1:38."

- Then that child starts the ball around the circle again, beginning with the rest of the Scripture, "Let it be with me just as you have said."

- After a few rounds, play the game using the word "me" as the keyword. Whoever is holding the ball when the Scripture gets to the word "me," must call out, "Luke 1:38!"

Sign the Verse

- Have the children sit down.

- Teach the children signs from American Sign Language for the keywords of today's Bible verse.

- Say the verse with the children, signing the keywords.

Prepare

✓ Photocopy and cut apart the Nazareth map (page 15, bottom) for each child.

✓ Use a marker to write each letter of the name NAZARETH on a separate piece of paper.

✓ Place the letters on the floor in a circle (like you were making the circle for a cake walk). Make a circle for every eight children.

Prepare

✓ Provide a CEB Bible and a ball.

I am—Point to self.

Lord's—Make an "L" with the right hand. Place the "L" at the left shoulder and then move across the body to the right waist.

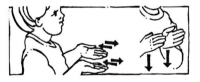
Servant—Hold both hands palms up. Alternate moving your hands back and forth in front of your body. Hold both hands in front of your body with palms facing each other. Bring both hands straight down.

Me—Point to self.

You—Point to others.

Say—Hold your index finger at your chin. Move finger forward and down.

Small Groups

Divide the children into small groups. You may organize the groups around age levels or around readers and nonreaders. Keep the groups small, with a maximum of ten children in each group. You may need to have more than one of each group.

Young Children

- Give each child the angel circle you cut out before class. Encourage the children to decorate the circles with crayons or markers.

- **Say:** Today our Bible story was about a young woman named Mary. Mary lived in a small town named Nazareth.

- Give each child a copy of the map of Palestine (page 17) and a large piece of construction paper.

- Show each child how to fold the construction paper in half to make a folder. Help each child write his or her name on the cover of the folder.

- Have the children glue the map on the inside of the folder.

- Help the children circle the name *Nazareth* on their maps.

- **Ask:** What happened to Mary in the Bible story? (*The angel Gabriel came to Mary with a message from God.*)

- Encourage the children to glue the angel circles somewhere on the edge of the maps.

- Help each child draw a line from the circle to Nazareth.

- **Ask:** How do you think Mary felt when she saw the angel? (*afraid*) What did the angel tell Mary? (*She would have a baby named Jesus.*)

- **Say:** When Mary heard that her baby was the Son of God, "Then Mary said, 'I am the Lord's servant. Let it be with me just as you have said.'" That's our Bible verse for today. Repeat it after me.

- Repeat the Bible verse and use the signs from page 11.

- **Say:** Mary might have been afraid, but she said she was willing to do what God wanted her to do.

- **Ask:** What are some things you think God wants you to do?

- Give each child a copy of the "Things God Wants Me to Do" list (page 18). Talk about each item on the list.

- **Say:** Like Mary, we can do what God wants us to do. Think about something you are willing to do this week.

- Help the children check the things they are willing to do this next week. Place the list in each child's folder and save until next week.

- Enjoy eating the bread made earlier with the children.

- **Pray:** Thank you, God, for bread. Thank you for Mary, who did what you wanted her to do. Help me do what you want me to do. Amen.

Prepare

✓ Photocopy the map circles (page 16), the map of Palestine (page 17), and the "Things God Wants Me to Do" list (page 18) for each child.

✓ Provide scissors, gluesticks, 12-by-18 construction paper, crayons or markers, napkins, and bread made earlier (page 8).

✓ Cut out a map circle of the angel (page 16) for each child.

Older Children

- Give the children the angel map circles. Have the children cut out the circles.

- Encourage the children to decorate the circles with colored pencils.

- **Say:** Today our Bible story was about a young woman named Mary. Mary lived in a small town named Nazareth.

- Give each child a copy of the map of Palestine (page 17) and a large piece of construction paper.

- Instruct each child to fold the construction paper in half to make a folder. Have each child write his or her name on the cover of the folder.

- Have the children glue the map on the inside of the folder.

- Help the children find and circle the name Nazareth on the maps.

- **Ask:** What happened to Mary in the Bible story? *(The angel Gabriel came to Mary with a message from God.)*

- Encourage the children to glue the angel circles somewhere on the edge of the maps.

- Give each child a length of yarn. Have the child glue the yarn from the circle to Nazareth.

- **Ask:** How do you think Mary felt when she saw the angel? *(afraid)* What did the angel tell Mary? *(She would have a baby named Jesus.)*

- **Say:** When Mary heard that her baby was the Son of God, "Then Mary said, 'I am the Lord's servant. Let it be with me just as you have said.'" That's our Bible verse for today. Let's look it up in our Bibles.

- Help the children find Luke 1:38 in their CEB Bibles. Have the children read the Bible verse with you.

- **Say:** Mary might have been afraid, but she said she was willing to do what God wanted her to do.

- **Ask:** What are some things you think God wants you to do?

- Give each child the "Things God Wants Me to Do" list (page 18). Talk about each item on the list.

- **Say:** Like Mary, we can do what God wants us to do. Think about something you are willing to do this week.

- Help the children check the things they are willing to do this next week. Place the list in each child's folder and save until next week.

- Enjoy eating the bread made earlier with the children.

- **Pray:** Thank you, God, for bread. Thank you for a young woman named Mary, who did what you wanted her to do. Help me do what you want me to do. Amen.

Prepare

✓ Photocopy the map circles (page 16), the map of Palestine (page 17), and the "Things God Wants Me to Do" list (page 18) for each child.

✓ Provide CEB Bibles, scissors, gluesticks, 12-by-18 construction paper, colored pencils, yarn, napkins, and bread made earlier (page 8).

The Lord
is with you!

The Lord
is with you!

The Lord
is with you!

The Lord
is with you!

The Journey: Walking the Road to Bethlehem Children's Edition

I am the Lord's servant.
(Luke 1:38, CEB)

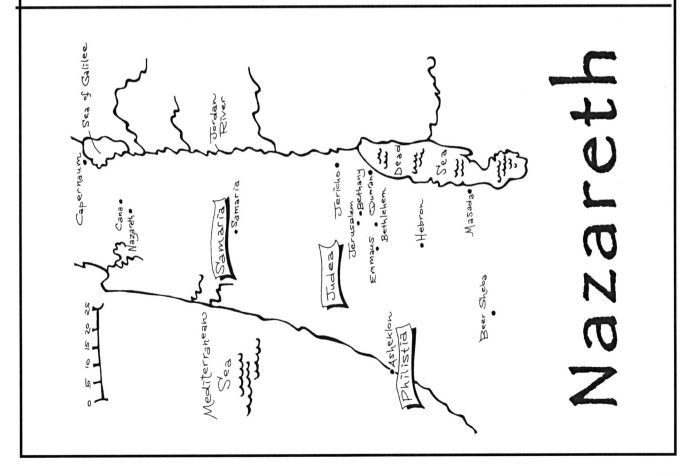

Nazareth

The Journey: Walking the Road to Bethlehem Children's Edition

Capernaum
Sea of Galilee

Cana
Nazareth

Mediterranean
Sea

Samaria
Samaria

Jordan
River

Judea
Jericho
Jerusalem
Bethany
Ein karem
Qumran
Bethlehem

Ashkelon
Dead
Philistia
Hebron
Sea
Masada

Beer Sheba

0 5 10 15 20 25

Things God Wants Me to Do

❑ Love God

❑ Love others

❑ Bring an offering

❑ Pray

❑ Read the Bible

❑ Go to church

❑ Care for God's world

❑ Share

The Journey: Walking the Road to Bethlehem Children's Edition

Now Appearing at Nazareth

by Daphna Flegal

(Gabriel swoops in, holding his arms out wide. He moves among the children while shouting) Rejoice, favored ones! The Lord is with you! *(Repeat several times.)*

(Gabriel stops by the well.)

(Still shouting) Don't be afraid; I'm not here to scare you.

(Thoughtfully) Although, I'm sure having an angel drop by might be a little frightening. I mean, how often do you get to see an angel?

(Quietly) Anyway, don't be afraid. Let me introduce myself. I'm the angel Gabriel, a messenger from God.

(Normal voice) And I've come to tell you some exciting news. "What news is that?" you ask. *(Pause)* I said, you ask "What news is that?" *(Get the children to say, "What news is that?")* I'm so glad you asked. It is really great news. In fact, it is the best news ever. I mean, this is fantastically awesome, stupendously marvelous news. A young woman is going to have a baby. Yep, that's it. That's the news. A young woman is having a baby. "So, what?" you ask. *(Pause)* I said, you ask "So, what?" *(Get the children to say, "So, what?")* I'm so glad you asked. Let me tell you all about it.

A young woman named Mary lives in the small town of Nazareth. She's just an ordinary girl, living in an ordinary small town. She's engaged to be married to a man named Joseph, but right now she's still living at home, doing all the things a young woman is supposed to do. She bakes bread, she sweeps the floor, she goes to the well for water. *(Point to well.)*

One day I *(Jump forward)* suddenly appeared before her and said *(Shouting)*, "Rejoice, favored one! The Lord is with you!"

(Normal voice) I may have gotten a little carried away with the suddenly-appeared part, because she was obviously afraid.

(Quiet voice) I tried to calm her fears. "Don't be afraid, Mary," I said. "God is pleased with you. You're going to have a baby, a son, and you shall name him Jesus. He will grow up to be great and he will be called the Son of the Most High."

(Normal voice) "How can that be?" you ask. *(Pause)* I said, you ask "How can that be?" *(Get the children to say, "How can that be?")* I'm so glad you asked. I'll tell you what I told Mary. God's Spirit will make it happen. Remember, nothing is impossible for God.

Mary was quiet for a long time. I could tell she was thinking about what I had told her. Finally, she spoke. "What did she say?" you ask. *(Pause)* I said, you ask "What did she say?" *(Get the children to say, "What did she say?")* I'm so glad you asked.

(Quiet voice) Then Mary said, "I am the Lord's servant. Let it be with me just as you have said."

2 Joseph

Objectives

The children will
- hear Matthew 1:18-24.
- discover that another name we can call Jesus is *Emmanuel*; and that *Emmanuel* means "God with us."
- learn how Joseph responded to God.
- explore ways they can respond to God.

Bible Story

Matthew 1:18-24, CEB: Gabriel comes to Joseph in a dream.

Bible Verse

Matthew 1:23, CEB: *And they will call him,* Emmanuel. (*Emmanuel* means "God with us.")

Focus for the Teacher

Who Was Joseph?

Joseph was a carpenter. In New Testament times, carpenters could be woodworkers, craftsmen, or stonemasons. Carpenters repaired plows, made the beams that held up the flat roofs, and built wooden doors and door frames. Skilled carpenters made intricate cabinets and chests, as well as tables and yokes.

> *And they will call him,* Emmanuel. (*Emmanuel* means "God with us.")
> Matthew 1:23, CEB

Joseph was probably a young man of New Testament times. He was likely the same age as any young man ready to be married. This would make him about fourteen or fifteen years old.

Joseph was a kind man. The Gospel of Matthew tells us that Mary and Joseph were already engaged when Mary learns that she is pregnant. Engagements in New Testament times were as binding as marriage, and could only be broken by divorce or death. When Joseph learns of Mary's pregnancy, he decides to quietly divorce her rather than have her put to death.

Joseph was obedient to God. When an angel comes to Joseph in a dream, Joseph follows the angel's directions. He goes ahead with the marriage to Mary and names the baby Jesus. Like Mary, Joseph's response was to trust God.

The Bible Verse

The word *Emmanuel* is a Hebrew word meaning "God with us." This verse refers back to the Old Testament Scripture found in Isaiah 7:14. Matthew uses this passage to show his readers that Jesus fulfills the Scriptures. "God with us" means that Jesus is truly divine (God), but also fully human (with us).

Bethlehem

Bethlehem was Joseph's hometown. The Gospel of Matthew tells us that Joseph was living in Bethlehem when he became engaged to Mary. Bethlehem was about six miles from Jerusalem. In Jesus' time, Bethlehem was home to workers who made their living by farming, taking care of sheep, building and carpentry, and baking.

The name *Bethlehem* means "house of bread," probably because grains were grown there and they were used to bake bread that could be smelled all around the city.

Explore Interest Groups

Be sure that adult leaders are waiting when the first child arrives. Greet and welcome each child. Get the child involved in an activity that interests him or her and introduces the theme for the day's activities.

A Carpenter's Angel

- Recruit an adult or teenager to dress as an angel (with or without wings) to greet each child as she or he enters the room.

- **The angel says:** Look, *(child's name)*! Mary will have a son. They will call him *Emmanuel,* which means "God with us."

- Give each child a piece of sandpaper and a copy of the angel pattern (page 28).

- Show the child how to trace the angel onto the back of the sandpaper.

- Have the child cut out the angel using safety scissors. Precut the angels for younger children.

- Give each child a cinnamon stick. Show the children how to rub the sticks across the rough side of the sandpaper.

- Help each child use a paper punch to punch a hole in the top of the angel.

- Show each child how to tie a piece of ribbon through the hole to make a hanger.

- Write each child's name on the smooth side of his or her angel.

- **Say:** Today carpenters use sandpaper to rub over wood and make the wood smooth. Our Bible story is about a Bible-times carpenter named Joseph. While Joseph was sleeping, God sent an angel to talk to Joseph in his dreams. The angel told Joseph that Mary would have a baby named Jesus.

The Carpenter's Shop

- Invite the children to experience Joseph's carpenter shop in Bethlehem.

- Set up woodworking stations. These may be as simple or as elaborate as you wish. You can simply set supplies on a table or decorate the area to be a carpenter's shop.

- Invite adults who enjoy woodworking to visit and show the children how to safely use the tools.

Sand

- Cover the workspace with recycled newspapers. Place wood scraps and various grits of sandpaper in the station. Choose scraps without splinters.

Prepare

- ✓ Recruit an adult or teenager to portray an angel.

- ✓ Photocopy the angel pattern (page 28) for each child.

- ✓ Provide newspapers, sandpaper, safety scissors, cinnamon sticks, ribbon, a paper punch, and markers.

- ✓ Use the angel pattern to precut angels from sandpaper for younger children.

- ✓ Cover the table with recycled newspapers.

Prepare

- ✓ Provide newspapers, wood scraps, and sandpaper in a variety of grits.

- ✓ Cover the table with recycled newspapers.

- Show the children how to use the sandpaper to smooth the rough edges of the scraps. Let the children feel the different grits of sandpaper.

- **Say:** Today our Bible story is about a man named Joseph. Joseph was a carpenter. He worked with wood.

Hammer

- Place a large piece of wood on a sturdy table or on the floor.

- Show the children how to hammer large nails in the wood. Start off the nail for each child. Always have adult supervision as the children use hammers.

- If you choose not to use hammers and nails, provide sheets of plastic foam and golf tees. Push the golf tee into the foam to get the "nail" started. Let the children use wooden mallets or toy hammers to hammer the golf tees into the foam.

- **Say:** Today our Bible story is about a man named Joseph. Joseph was a carpenter in Bible times. He would have cut and hammered wood to build furniture, like tables and stools.

Prepare

✓ Provide a large piece of wood, hammers, and large nails; or pieces of plastic foam, golf tees, and mallets or toy hammers.

Glue

- Place wood scraps and wood glue in this station. Let the children use wood glue to glue the scraps together however they wish.

- **Say:** Today our Bible story is about a man named Joseph. Joseph was a carpenter in Bible times. He would have made tools, such as plows and yokes. He would have helped build doors and stairs for houses.

Prepare

✓ Provide wood scraps and wood glue.

✓ Cover the table with recycled newspapers.

Measure

- Encourage the children to make Bible-times measuring sticks.

- Give each child two 10-inch pieces of lathe and a piece of sandpaper. Have the children sand the edges of each piece.

- Have older children mark one end of each strip about ½ inch in from the edge. Help the children use hand drills to drill holes on the marks. Pre-drill the holes for younger children.

- Have each child use a forefinger to measure across both pieces of lathe. Mark each measurement with a permanent, fine-tip marker.

- **Say:** This unit of measure is called a finger. It is about ¾ of an inch long.

- Give each child a piece of string or leather lacing. Tie the two lathe strips together with the lacing to form a measuring stick.

- Have each child find a partner. Let the partners use their measuring sticks to measure each other. How many fingers tall is each child?

- **Say:** Joseph was a carpenter in Bible times. He would have used measuring sticks to help him build.

Prepare

✓ Provide newspapers, 1-inch-wide lathe strips cut 10 inches long (two per child), sandpaper, permanent fine-tip markers, hand drills, pencils, and string or leather lacing.

✓ Pre-drill the hole for younger children.

✓ Cover the table with recycled newspapers.

Sawdust Sculpture

- Invite the children to help you mix together sawdust dough.

- Mix together 2 cups clean sawdust and 1 cup flour into a large mixing bowl. Add water until the mixture holds together in a stiff dough.

- Give each child a piece of wax paper and a lump of sawdust dough. Encourage the children to play with the dough—roll it, pound it, shape it, and reshape it.

- Invite the children to make angel ornaments with their dough.

- Have the children flatten the clay until it is a slab about ¼ inch thick.

- Help each child use a cookie cutter to make an angel in the dough. Show the child how to tear away the extra dough.

- Punch a hole in the top of each ornament with an unsharpened pencil.

- Set the angels aside to dry.

Prepare

✓ Provide wax paper, clean sawdust (available at hardware stores), flour, water, large mixing bowl, measuring cups, mixing spoon, angel cookie cutters, and an unsharpened pencil.

Great Artists at Work

- **Say:** A famous painting showing Joseph and the angel was done by Georges de La Tour. This artist was born in France in the late 1500s. He painted with dark shadows and limited colors. He was also well known for having candlelight in his paintings.

- Show the children *The Dream of St. Joseph* by Georges de La Tour. Point out the candle and the colors.

- **Say:** The Bible does not tell us how old Joseph was when he became engaged to Mary. In this painting, the artist has made Joseph older, but Joseph might have been around age fifteen, the age when most New Testament men married.

- Give each child a piece of drawing paper. Let the children use pencils to sketch a painting of Joseph and the angel. Encourage the children to add a candle to their paintings.

- Let the children choose various shades of one color paint, crayons, or colored pencils to add monochromatic color to their sketches.

- Save the paintings for an art show in Lesson 5.

Prepare

✓ Provide newspapers or a plastic tablecloth; large drawing paper; pencils; paint smocks; washable paints and brushes, crayons, or colored pencils.

✓ Cover the table with newspapers or a plastic tablecloth. If you use paint, have the children wear smocks.

✓ Provide a copy of *The Dream of St. Joseph* by Georges de La Tour. Search online or in the library for images of the painting.

Do the Opposite

- Have the children stand in a circle in an open area of the room.

- **Say:** Today's Bible story is about Joseph. Joseph was a good man. He followed the rules and laws. But after he heard the angel's message, he had to do the opposite of what was expected.

  Let's play a game of opposites. I want you to do the opposite of everything I say. Stand up. Sit down. Stand on both feet. Stand on one foot. Stand very still. Wiggle all over.

Large Group

Bring all the children together to experience the Bible story. Use jingle bells to alert the children to the large-group time.

Are You Sleeping?

- Have the children form a line at one end of an open area. Place a chair on the other end of the area. This is where Joseph will sleep.

- **Say:** In our Bible story today, God sends an angel to give Joseph a message while Joseph is sleeping. Let's pretend we are the angel. We will try to sneak up on Joseph and deliver the message. We'll call out, "Joseph, are you sleeping?" If Joseph snores, then we can get a step closer. If he answers "No!," then we have to scramble back to the line. If Joseph catches one of us before we get back to the line, that person becomes Joseph.

- Select one child to be Joseph. Joseph sits in the chair and responds to the question. Play the game until most of the children have had a chance to be Joseph.

Now Appearing at Bethlehem

- Recruit an adult or teenager to portray Joseph. Give the actor a photocopy of the script (page 29) and provide a costume, a piece of wood, and a hammer.

- Have the children sit down in the large-group area.

- Have Joseph tell the story "Life Is But a Dream" to the children (page 29).

Bethlehem Squares

- Use masking tape to create a large ticktacktoe grid on the floor. If you have a large group of children, divide the children into groups of nine and create a grid for each group.

- Divide the children into two teams: the Xs and the Os.

- **Say:** Let's review what we know about Bethlehem. I will ask each team a true-or-false question. If your team answers the question correctly, one member of your team will stand on a square of the ticktacktoe board. If your team answers the question incorrectly, your team loses the turn. When your team has three people standing in a row or in a diagonal line, your team wins.

- **Questions**
  1. The name *Bethlehem* means "house of bread." *(true)*
  2. Joseph was a tax collector in Bethlehem. *(false)*
  3. Baby Jesus was born in Nazareth. *(false)*
  4. Joseph had to travel to Bethlehem because of the census. *(true)*

Prepare

✓ Recruit an adult or teenager to portray Joseph.

✓ Photocopy the script (page 29) for the actor.

✓ Provide a costume, piece of wood, and hammer.

Prepare

✓ Provide masking tape.

5. Bethlehem was the home of King David. (*true*)
6. The star led the wise men to Bethlehem. (*true*)
7. Joseph was a carpenter from Bethlehem. (*true*)
8. Angels came to shepherds who were watching their goats on a hillside in Bethlehem. (*false*)
9. Joseph had to go to Bethlehem because he was from David's family. (*true*)

Bonus: Spell Bethlehem.

Bible Verse

• Teach the children to sing the first part of the Bible verse to the tune of "God Is So Good."

> They will call him,
> They will call him,
> They will call him,
> E-e mman-u-el.

• Then teach the children to sing the second part of the verse to the tune of "London Bridge."

> Emmanuel means "God with us."
> "God with us." "God with us."
> Emmanuel means "God with us."
> God is with us.

• Divide the children into two groups. Have group one sing the first part of the verse. Have group two sing the second part of the verse.

• **Say:** When I point to your group, stand up and sing your part of the verse. Then sit back down.

• Point to the first group. Have them stand and sing. Then point to the second group. The first group sits down, and the second group stands and sings.

• Continue pointing, mixing up which group you are pointing to. You might point to group 1, group 2, group 2, group 1, group 1, group 1, group 1, group 2.

Sign and Spell

• Use the manual alphabet (page 29) to teach the children the signs for the letters "e," "m," "a," "n," "u," and "l."

• Shout the following cheer and have the children respond by shouting and signing the letter.

• Give me an "E." (*Sign and say "E."*) Give me an "m." (*Sign and say "m."*) Give me another "m." (*Sign and say "m."*) Give me an "a." (*Sign and say "a."*) Give me an "n." (*Sign and say "n."*) Give me a "u." (*Sign and say "u."*) Give me an "e." (*Sign and say "e."*) Give me an "l." (*Sign and say "l."*) What does that spell? (*Emmanuel*) What does that spell? (*Emmanuel*) And what does that mean? (*God with us!*)

Prepare

✓ Photocopy the manual alphabet (page 29).

Small Groups

Divide the children into small groups. You may organize the groups around age levels or around readers and nonreaders. Keep the groups small, with a maximum of ten children in each group. You may need to have more than one of each group.

Young Children

- Give each child the Joseph circle you cut out before class. Encourage the children to decorate the circles with crayons or markers.

- **Say:** Today our Bible story was about a man named Joseph. Joseph lived in a town named Bethlehem.

- Give each child his or her map-of-Palestine folder. Help the children circle the name *Bethlehem* on their maps.

- **Ask:** What happened to Joseph in the Bible story? *(An angel came to Joseph in a dream.)*

- Encourage the children to glue the Joseph circles somewhere on the edge of the maps.

- Help each child draw a line from the circle to Bethlehem.

- **Ask:** How do you think Joseph felt when he woke up from his dream? What did the angel tell Joseph? *(Mary would have God's Son.)* The angel told Joseph to name the baby Jesus. The angel said that Jesus would also be called by another name. What was that name? *(Emmanuel)* What does *Emmanuel* mean? *(God with us.)*

- Hold open the Bible to Matthew 1:23. Say the verse with the children: "*And they will call him,* Emmanuel. (*Emmanuel* means 'God with us.')."

- **Say:** When Joseph heard the angel's message, he obeyed God. Joseph was willing to do what God wanted him to do.

- Give each child the "Things God Wants Me to Do" list from Lesson 1.

- **Ask:** Did you do the things you said you were willing to do? Are there things you are willing to do again?

- Affirm any children who followed through with the list. Encourage children who did not follow through to try again this week. Place the list back in each child's folder.

- Invite the children to sit in a circle on the floor. Place a basket of grapes and raisins in the center of the circle.

- **Say:** Joseph probably ate grapes and raisins similar to these. Bible-times people sat on mats on the floor to eat. They did not use individual plates or forks. Instead, everyone ate from the same bowl or basket.

- Enjoy eating the grapes and raisins with the children.

- **Pray:** Thank you, God, for grapes and raisins. Thank you for Joseph, who did what you wanted him to do. Help me do what you want me to do. Amen.

Prepare

- ✓ Photocopy the map circles (page 16), the map of Palestine (page 17), and the "Things God Wants Me to Do" list (page 18) for any child absent for Lesson 1.

- ✓ Provide a CEB Bible, the map folders from Lesson 1 (page 12), safety scissors, pencils, gluesticks, crayons or markers, napkins, and a basket of grapes and raisins.

- ✓ Cut out a map circle of Joseph for each child (page 16).

Older Children

- Give the children the Joseph map circles. Have the children cut out the circles.

- Encourage the children to decorate the circles with colored pencils.

- **Say:** Today our Bible story was about a man named Joseph. Joseph lived in a town named Bethlehem.

- Give each child her or his map-of-Palestine folder. Help the children circle the name *Bethlehem* on their maps.

- **Ask:** What happened to Joseph in the Bible story? *(An angel came to Joseph in a dream.)*

- Encourage the children to glue the Joseph circles somewhere on the edge of the maps.

- Give each child a length of yarn. Have the child glue the yarn from the circle to Bethlehem.

- **Ask:** How do you think Joseph felt when he woke up from his dream? What did the angel tell Joseph? *(Mary would have God's Son.)*

- **Say:** The angel told Joseph to name the baby Jesus. The angel said that Jesus would also be called by another name. What was that name? *(Emmanuel)* What does *Emmanuel* mean? *(God with us.)*

- Help the children find Matthew 1:23 in their CEB Bibles. Have the children read the Bible verse with you.

- **Say:** When Joseph heard the angel's message, he obeyed God. Joseph was willing to do what God wanted him to do.

- Give each child the "Things God Wants Me to Do" list from Lesson 1 (page 18).

- **Ask:** Did you do the things you said you were willing to do? Are there things you are willing to do again?

- Affirm any children who followed through with the list. Encourage children who did not follow through to try again this week. Place the list back in each child's folder.

- Invite the children to sit in a circle on the floor. Place a basket of grapes and raisins in the center of the circle.

- **Say:** Joseph probably ate grapes and raisins similar to these. Bible-times people sat on mats on the floor to eat. They did not use individual plates or forks. Instead, everyone ate from the same bowl or basket.

- Enjoy eating the grapes and raisins with the children.

- **Pray:** Thank you, God, for grapes and raisins. Thank you for Joseph, who did what you wanted him to do. Help me do what you want me to do. Amen.

Prepare

✓ Photocopy the map circles (page 16), the map of Palestine (page 17), and the "Things God Wants Me to Do" list (page 18) for any child absent for Lesson 1.

✓ Provide CEB Bibles, the map folders from Lesson 1 (page 12), safety scissors, colored pencils, glue, yarn, napkins, and a basket of grapes and raisins.

The Journey: Walking the Road to Bethlehem Children's Edition

Life Is But a Dream

by Daphna Flegal

(Joseph enters and starts hammering on a piece of wood. While he is hammering, he sings "Row, Row, Row, Your Boat." After singing, "Life is but a dream," he stops hammering and looks at the audience.)

Oh, greetings, my young carpenter apprentices. Are you ready to begin today's lesson? I'm going to teach you how to make a table. First, you must choose the right kind of wood.

(Joseph picks up the wood and starts to sing "Row, Row, Row Your Boat" again. Joseph stops singing in the middle of the song.)

What? Oh, why yes, I am in a good mood. In fact, I'm in a very good mood. I know, I know. I've been moping about for a few days, but that's all changed. Now *(singing)* life is but a dream…

What's happened? Well, let's sit down for a minute and I'll tell you. *(Joseph sits.)*

You know I am engaged to Mary, right? Well, a few days ago she comes to me and says, "Joseph, I've got some important news." Then she tells me that an angel came to her and told her she was going to have a baby—and that the baby was God's Son! I mean, she was serious. She believed what she was saying. But really, an angel just shows up one day in Nazareth? How could I believe *that*?

At first, I was angry. Then I was just sad. How could Mary do this to me? I knew I was not the father of the baby, but who was? The law says I could have Mary put to death, but I didn't want to hurt Mary. So I decided to divorce her. It was better that way.

I was still feeling sad when I went to bed that night. At first, I couldn't go to sleep; I kept thinking about Mary. But finally, my eyes closed and I fell asleep. Then I had this dream… *(Joseph leans back and closes his eyes, as if going to sleep.)* It was a good dream.

An angel from God came to *me*. An angel spoke to *me*.

"Don't be afraid to take Mary as your wife," said the angel. "The baby is God's Son. His name is Jesus. He will also be called Emmanuel, which means God with us."

(Joseph opens his eyes and sits up.) When I woke up, I knew what Mary had told me was true. Mary's baby was God's Son! I was going to help take care of God's Son. Wow! Maybe I'll teach him to be a carpenter too.

So, that's why I'm in such a good mood. I'm having a baby boy. I'm going to name him Jesus. Hey, I know. Instead of a table, let's make a cradle. I'll go get some more wood. *(Joseph begins singing "Row, Row, Row Your Boat" again as he exits.)*

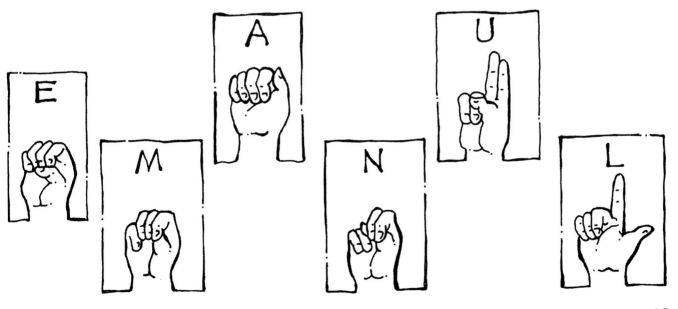

3 Elizabeth

Objectives
The children will
- hear Luke 1:39-56.
- learn that Elizabeth welcomed Mary with joy.
- hear the Magnificat, Mary's song of praise to God.
- have the opportunity to praise God for the gift of Jesus.

Bible Story
Luke 1:39-56, NRSV: Mary visits Elizabeth.

Bible Verse
Luke 1:46-47, NRSV: My soul magnifies the Lord, and my spirit rejoices in God my Savior.

Focus for the Teacher

Cousin Elizabeth

Elizabeth was an older relative of Mary. She was married to Zechariah, a priest serving at the Temple in Jerusalem. Elizabeth and Zechariah were older and had no children, a tragedy in Bible times. But like the stories of Sarah and Hannah, God intervened. One day during Zechariah's priestly duties, the angel Gabriel appeared to him with the message that Elizabeth would have a child who would be great in the sight of the Lord. Zechariah expressed doubt and, because of his disbelief, was struck mute until the day his son was born. Elizabeth and Zechariah's son grew up to be John the Baptist.

After Gabriel's visit, Mary went to Elizabeth who was now about six months pregnant. Mary traveled nine days on foot to be with her older relative. When Mary arrived at Elizabeth's home, the child in Elizabeth's womb leapt with joy. Elizabeth accepts and encourages Mary, reminding Mary that she is blessed.

Mary stayed with Elizabeth until just before the birth of John. Surely, she and Elizabeth discussed their concerns and their joys as they did the household tasks. Elizabeth probably acted as a mentor to Mary, and Mary brought Elizabeth youthful joy.

> My soul magnifies the Lord, and my spirit rejoices in God my Savior.
>
> Luke 1:46-47, NRSV

The Bible Verse

Today's Bible verse is called the Magnificat. It is a great hymn of praise and refers to Hannah's song of praise in 1 Samuel 2:1-10. While the song is definitely a song of praise, it is also a song of revolution—the revolution of God, where the lowly are lifted up and the hungry are filled with good things. Mary's words tell of God's redeeming work through God's Son, Jesus.

Ein Karem

Since the early centuries of the Christian faith, the village of Ein Karem has been associated with Elizabeth's home and the place Mary came to visit her. Today a church marks the traditional site of the birthplace of John the Baptist. We don't know for certain that John was actually born here, but we do know that it has been his traditional birthplace for over seventeen hundred years.

The village grew up around a spring, and it's name means "the spring of the vineyard." It was in the foothills of the Judea Mountains and was surrounded by vineyards and olive groves. It was close enough to Jerusalem that Zechariah could travel to the Temple to perform his priestly duties.

Explore Interest Groups

Be sure that adult leaders are waiting when the first child arrives. Greet and welcome each child. Get the child involved in an activity that interests him or her and introduces the theme for the day's activities. The children will need the rattles made in "Preparing for Babies" during large-group time.

Blessings

- Recruit an older adult to dress as Elizabeth to greet each child as he or she enters the room. This person will also tell the story as Elizabeth during large-group time.

- **Elizabeth says:** Greetings, *(child's name)*. God has blessed you.

- Invite the children to the activity table to make blessing strips.

- **Say:** Today our Bible story is about Mary and her older relative Elizabeth. After the angel told Mary that she would have God's Son, he told her that Elizabeth was also having a baby. Mary left Nazareth and went to stay with Elizabeth. When Elizabeth saw Mary, she knew that Mary's baby was special. Elizabeth told Mary that God had blessed her.

- **Ask:** What does it mean when we say someone is blessed? *(something nice has happened to that person)* How do we usually respond when something nice happens to us or when someone does something nice for you? *(We are thankful.)*

- **Say:** God has done something nice for each one of us. God has given us a great gift. The gift is Jesus.

- Give each child the cut-apart copies of the five blessing strips (page 38). Have each child write his or her name on each strip.

- Show the children the strip with the name Jesus.

- **Say:** Jesus shows us how much God loves us.

- **Ask:** What are some other blessings God gives to us? *(family, friends, food, love, sun, rain, animals, homes)*

- Show the children the remaining strips. Encourage the children to decorate the strips with crayons or markers.

- Let the children make strips out of blank paper to add more blessings.

- Save the blessing strips to use during the weaving activity.

Welcome to Ein Karem

- Invite the children to experience Elizabeth's home in Ein Karem.

- Set up different "home" stations. These may be as simple or as elaborate as you wish. You can simply set supplies on a table or decorate the area to be Bible-times homes.

Prepare

- ✓ Photocopy and cut apart the five blessing strips (page 38) for each child.

- ✓ Provide crayons or markers, scissors, and blank paper.

- ✓ Recruit an older adult to portray Elizabeth.

- ✓ Provide a costume for Elizabeth.

Weaving

- **Say:** Mary traveled for nine days to visit Elizabeth. She stayed with Elizabeth for about three months. Mary and Elizabeth probably did the normal things women in Bible times did every day. Women in Bible times made the clothing needed for their families. But before they could make a robe or a tunic, they had to spin the wool to make thread and then they had to weave the thread together to make cloth. In Bible times, spinning was considered women's work, but weaving was done by both men and women.

- Give each child a piece of burlap that you have prepared for weaving.

- Show the children how to start at the top of the burlap with the open spaces running up and down. The burlap makes the warp threads.

- Have the children weave a blessing strip under and over the warp threads. They continue this under-over pattern until they reach the other side.

- Have the children add strips until the mat is full.

Prepare

- ✓ Provide burlap, blessing strips made earlier (page 31), and scissors.

- ✓ Cut burlap into 8-by-11 rectangles for each child. Pull the strings from each piece of burlap to open the lines for weaving.

Cooking

- Have the children wash their hands.

- **Say:** Today our Bible story is about Mary and her older relative Elizabeth. Elizabeth lived in a town called Ein Karem. The name means "spring of the vineyard." Grapes were grown in vineyards. In Bible times, grapes were eaten, dried into raisins, or made into wine. Let's use raisins to make a snack. The snack is similar to Halvah Balls, a treat they would have eaten in Bible times.

- Let the children pour the chopped raisins, dates, and apricots into a large mixing bowl. Add the cinnamon and lemon zest. Mix the ingredients together. Add enough lemon juice so that the mixture sticks together.

- Show the children how to roll the mixture into balls. Place the balls on wax paper.

- Save the Halvah Balls to eat during small-group time.

- **Say:** Mary traveled for nine days to visit Elizabeth. She stayed with Elizabeth for about three months. Mary and Elizabeth probably cooked together during Mary's stay.

Preparing for Babies

- **Say:** Mary stayed with Elizabeth for about three months. They probably spent a lot of time talking about their babies and getting ready for their babies to be born.

- **Ask:** What do we do today to get ready for babies? *(prepare a nursery, buy or make clothes, buy toys)*

Prepare

- ✓ Provide a plastic tablecloth, hand-washing supplies, wax paper, raisins, dates, dried apricots, cinnamon, lemon zest, lemon juice, large mixing bowl, measuring cups and spoons, mixing spoon, cookie sheets.

- ✓ Cover the table with a plastic tablecloth. Use a blender or food processor to chop the dates, apricots, and raisins.

Halvah Balls (without nuts)
4 oz dates, pitted
4 oz dried apricots
½ cup raisins
½ teaspoon cinnamon
1-2 tablespoons lemon juice
1-2 teaspoons lemon zest

- **Say:** Mary and Elizabeth probably did some of the same things. In Bible times, babies did not have nurseries, but they did have toys. Archaeologists have found baby toys at digs in Bible lands. These toys include whistles, rattles, wheeled animals, hoops, and spinning tops. Babies in Bible times, just like babies today, played with rattles. Some rattles were shaped like boxes.

- Let the children make rattles out of small boxes.

- Give each child a box. Have the children place pebbles or aquarium gravel inside the boxes. Securely tape the boxes closed.

- Let the children decorate the outside of the boxes to look like clay artifacts.

- Have the children tear off small pieces of masking tape and completely cover their boxes with pieces of tape. Rub over the tape to make the edges smooth against the box.

- Rub over the masking tape with the side of a brown crayon.

- Plan to use the rattles in large-group time.

Great Artists at Work

- **Say:** Rogier van der Weyden was a Dutch painter. He lived in the 1400s. He is known for painting triptychs. A triptych has three panels. They were often used on the altar in churches. Van der Weyden painted a polyptych of the birth of Jesus. A polyptych has many panels. He painted Mary's visit with Elizabeth on one of the panels.

- Show the children *Polyptych with the Nativity* by van der Weyden.

- Give each child a copy of the triptych panels pattern (page 39). Have the children trace the triptych onto posterboard. Let older children cut out the triptych themselves. Precut the triptychs for younger children.

- Show the children how to fold the triptychs to make them stand.

- **Say:** In our Bible story, Mary visits her older relative Elizabeth. It takes Mary nine days to walk to Elizabeth's house.

- **Ask:** How do you think Mary looked when she arrived at Elizabeth's house? How do you think Elizabeth looked when she saw Mary?

- **Say:** Design your triptych to tell today's Bible story. Where will you draw Mary? Where will you draw Elizabeth? Mary would not have traveled by herself. Do you want to include people traveling with Mary? Do you want to include Elizabeth's house? Elizabeth lived in a town called Ein Karem. The name means "spring of the vineyard." Grapes were grown in vineyards. Do you want to include vineyards or grapes?

- Encourage the children to draw and color or paint their triptychs.

- Save the triptychs for an art show in Lesson 5.

Prepare

✓ Provide small boxes such as gift boxes or individual cereal boxes, pebbles or aquarium gravel, masking tape, and brown crayons.

Prepare

✓ Photocopy the triptych pattern (page 39) for each child. Use the pattern to precut the triptychs for younger children.

✓ Provide newspapers or plastic tablecloth; large drawing paper; pencils; paint smocks; washable paints and brushes, crayons, or colored pencils; safety scissors; posterboard.

✓ Cover the table with newspapers or plastic tablecloth. If you use paint, have the children wear smocks.

✓ Provide a copy of *Polyptych with the Nativity* by Rogier van der Weyden. Search the library for images or online at: *http://www.wikipaintings.org/en/rogier-van-der-weyden/polyptych-with-the-nativity.*

NOTE: Websites are constantly changing. Although these websites were checked at the time this book was edited, we recommend that you double-check the site to verify that it is still live and that it is still appropriate for children before doing the activity.

Large Group

Bring all the children together to experience the Bible story. Use jingle bells to alert the children to the large-group time.

Great Greetings

- Divide the children into at least two teams. Have the teams move to one side of the room.

- Choose children to be Elizabeth for each team. Have the Elizabeths stand on the opposite side of the room from their teams.

- **Say:** Mary walked nine days to get to Elizabeth's house. When she finally got there, Elizabeth greeted Mary with joy. In Bible times, people often greeted one another with a bow. As they bowed, they used their hands to touch the forehead, the lips, and the heart.

- Encourage the children to stand and practice the bow.

- **Say:** Let's pretend that we are going to see Elizabeth. I will tell you how to go—I may tell you to walk or run or hop. Move as fast as you can to your team's Elizabeth. When you reach Elizabeth, you are to bow, touching your forehead, your lips, and your heart. Elizabeth will return your bow and say, "You are blessed!" As soon as Elizabeth says, "You are blessed," move quickly back to your team and I will tell the next person how to go to Elizabeth.

- Begin the game. Vary the way you have each person move (skip, hop on one foot, walk backwards, crab walk, tiptoe, moonwalk, and so forth). At some point in the game, choose different children to portray Elizabeth.

Now Appearing at Ein Karem

- Have the children sit down in the large-group area. Give the children the baby rattles they made earlier (page 33).

- **Say:** We have a special visitor today. Her name is Elizabeth, and even though she is older, she is expecting a baby. She's very excited about the baby and I think it will be fun to let her know we're excited too. I want you to listen carefully to her story. Every time you hear her say the word *baby*, shake your rattles.

- Have Elizabeth tell the story "Baby Talk" to the children. Encourage the children to shake their rattles each time Elizabeth says *baby*.

An Amazing Race

- Divide the children into at least two teams. Team 1 will compete against Team 2 to see who finishes the race first. If you have a small group of children or only young children, do the race as one group.

- Set up two challenge stations (see page 40).

Prepare

- ✓ Recruit an older adult to portray Elizabeth.

- ✓ Photocopy the script (page 43) for the actor.

- ✓ Provide a costume and the rattles the children made earlier (page 33).

- Have the children start at the first sign, "Nazareth."

- **Say:** Mary walked for nine days to travel from her home in Nazareth to Elizabeth's home in Ein Karem. Let's take our own nine-days journey. We'll need to follow directions and look for clues along the way. We'll start at Nazareth.

- Point out the sign for Nazareth. Encourage the children to read the sign. If you have a group of younger children, read the sign to them.

- **Say:** Looks like we'll travel by caravan. Can anyone find a donkey?

- Let each team find a picture of the donkey with a bundle on its back, and read the challenge (Challenge 1).

- **Say:** Good job! The donkey is your first challenge.

- Explain the first challenge (see page 40). After the children finish the challenge, they should be at the "Judean Hills" sign.

- **Say:** Congratulations! You made it to the hill country in Judea. Mary traveled to these hills to get to Ein Karem. Look for the hills *(Clue 1)* to find your first clue.

- When they find the picture of the hills, read Clue 1 to the children.

- **Ask:** What do you think we should do? *(Find water.)* Great idea! Look for someplace where we can find water.

- Let the children find the picture of the well (Clue 2). As they look, have the children continue to push the box donkeys on their journey.

- **Say:** Good job! You found the well and your next clue, Clue 2.

- Read Clue 2 to the children from the well card.

- **Say:** We must be getting close; there are vineyards in Ein Karem. Does anyone see any grapes?

- Let the children find the picture of the grapes, as they keep moving the box donkeys, and then read the card and Challenge 2.

- Explain Challenge 2 (see page 40). After the children finish the challenge, they should be at the "Ein Karem" sign.

- **Say:** Congratulations! You have all made it to Ein Karem, the home of Elizabeth. Everyone sit down so we can say the Bible verse together.

Bible Verse

- Have the children sit in a circle. Say the Bible verse for the children.

- **Ask:** What does the word *magnify* mean? *(to make something look bigger)*

- Hand the Bible verse card to one child in the circle. Have the child use the magnifying glass to read the first word of the verse.

- Keep passing the Bible verse and magnifying glass around the circle until everyone has had a chance to read a word in the verse. Let young children hold the magnifying glass for you to read the words.

Prepare

✓ Provide for each team—
Donkey Station: large box without a lid, blanket, stuffed-cloth bundle, crayons, and tape;
Baby Station: markers and strips of cloth.

✓ Photocopy and cut apart the three signs (page 42). Mount the "Nazareth" sign in one corner of the room. Mount the "Ein Karem" sign in an opposite corner of the room. Mount the "Judean Hills" sign somewhere in between the other two signs.

✓ For each team, photocopy and cut apart the donkey's face (page 40) and the four cards (page 41). Place the copies of the donkey's face in Challenge Station 1. Hide the copies of the four cards (for each team) from page 41 around the room.

Prepare

✓ Provide a magnifying glass.

✓ Photocopy and cut out the Bible verse card (page 43, bottom).

Small Groups

Divide the children into small groups. You may organize the groups around age levels or around readers and nonreaders. Keep the groups small, with a maximum of ten children in each group. You may need to have more than one of each group.

Young Children

- Give each child the Elizabeth circle you cut out before class. Encourage the children to decorate the circles with crayons or markers.

- **Say:** Today our Bible story was about Mary's trip to Ein Karem.

- Give each child his or her map-of-Palestine folder. Help the children circle the name *Ein Karem* on their maps.

- **Ask:** Why did Mary go to Ein Karem? *(to see Elizabeth)*

- Encourage the children to glue the Elizabeth circles somewhere on the edge of the maps.

- Help each child draw a line from the circle to Ein Karem.

- **Ask:** How do you think Elizabeth felt when she saw Mary? *(She was happy.)* How do you think Mary felt? *(She was happy.)* What did Mary do to show how happy she was? *(sang a song of joy)*

- Hold open the Bible to Luke 1:46-47. Say the verse with the children, "My soul magnifies the Lord, and my spirit rejoices in God my Savior."

- **Say:** Our Bible verse is the song Mary sang to praise God.

- **Ask:** What are some ways we praise God? *(sing, pray, dance, draw pictures, play musical instruments, come to church, and so forth)*

- Give each child a piece of construction paper and the precut Bible verse. Let the children glue the Bible verse on the page however they wish.

- Show the children the precut pictures of musical instruments.

- **Say:** One way we praise God is with music.

- Encourage the children to choose pictures and then glue them around the Bible verse.

- Let the children add confetti to their pages. Give the children glue or gluesticks. Instruct them to place dots of glue all over their pages. It does not matter if the confetti spills over onto the pictures or verse.

- Place each picture in a shallow tray. Show each child how to sprinkle confetti all over the picture. Shake off the extra confetti.

- Let the children use their Bible verse pictures as place mats.

- Give each child a paper plate, and share the Halvah Balls made earlier.

- **Pray:** Thank you, God, for foods they ate in Bible times and foods we still eat today. Thank you for stories from the Bible that tell us about Jesus' birth. We praise you for the gift of Jesus. Amen.

Prepare

✓ Photocopy the map circles (page 16) and the map of Palestine (page 17) for any child absent for Lessons 1 and 2. Photocopy the Bible verse (page 38) for each child.

✓ Provide an NRSV Bible, the map folders from Lesson 1 (page 12), safety scissors, crayons or markers, pictures of musical instruments, pencils, shallow trays, construction paper, glue or gluesticks, confetti, paper plates, napkins, and the Halvah Balls made earlier (page 32).

✓ Cut out a map circle of Elizabeth (page 16) and the Bible verse (page 38) for each child.

✓ Cut out pictures of musical instruments from catalogs, on the Internet, or in old Sunday school curriculum.

Older Children

- Give the children the Elizabeth map circles. Have the children cut out the circles.

- Encourage the children to decorate the circles with colored pencils.

- **Say:** Today our Bible story was about Mary's trip to Ein Karem.

- Give each child his or her map-of-Palestine folder. Help the children circle the name *Ein Karem* on their maps.

- **Ask:** Why did Mary go to Ein Karem? *(to see Elizabeth)*

- Encourage the children to glue the Elizabeth circles somewhere on the edge of the maps.

- Give each child a length of yarn. Have the child glue the yarn from the circle to Ein Karem.

- **Ask:** How do you think Elizabeth felt when she saw Mary? *(She was happy.)* How do you think Mary felt? *(She was happy.)* What did Mary do to show how happy she was? *(sang a song of joy)*

- Hold open the NRSV Bible to Luke 1:46-47. Say the verse with the children, "My soul magnifies the Lord, and my spirit rejoices in God my Savior."

- **Say:** Our Bible verse is the song Mary sang to praise God.

- **Ask:** What are some ways we praise God? *(sing, pray, dance, draw pictures, play musical instruments, come to church, and so forth)*

- Give each child a piece of construction paper and a copy of the Bible verse (page 38). Have the children cut out the Bible verse and glue it on the page however they wish.

- **Say:** One way we praise God is with music.

- Encourage the children to draw pictures of musical instruments around the Bible verse.

- The children may also write praise words such as *praise, joy,* and *rejoice.*

- Let the children add confetti to their pages. Give the children glue or gluesticks. Instruct them to place dots of glue all over their pages. It does not matter if the confetti spills over onto the pictures or verse.

- Place each picture in a shallow tray. Show each child how to sprinkle confetti all over the picture. Shake off the extra confetti.

- Let the children use their Bible verse pictures as place mats.

- Give each child a paper plate, and share the Halvah Balls made earlier.

- **Pray:** Thank you, God, for foods they ate in Bible times and foods we still eat today. Thank you for stories from the Bible that tell us about Jesus' birth. We praise you for the gift of Jesus. Amen.

Prepare

✓ Photocopy the map circles (page 16) and the map of Palestine (page 17) for any child absent for Lessons 1 and 2. Photocopy the Bible verse (page 38) for each child.

✓ Provide an NRSV Bible, the map folders from Lesson 1 (page 12), safety scissors, colored pencils, yarn, construction paper, glue or gluesticks, confetti, shallow trays, paper plates, napkins, and the Halvah Balls made earlier (page 32).

Love

Jesus

Family

Friends

Food

My soul magnifies the Lord,
and my spirit rejoices in God my Savior.

Luke 1:46-47, NRSV

The Journey: Walking the Road to Bethlehem Children's Edition

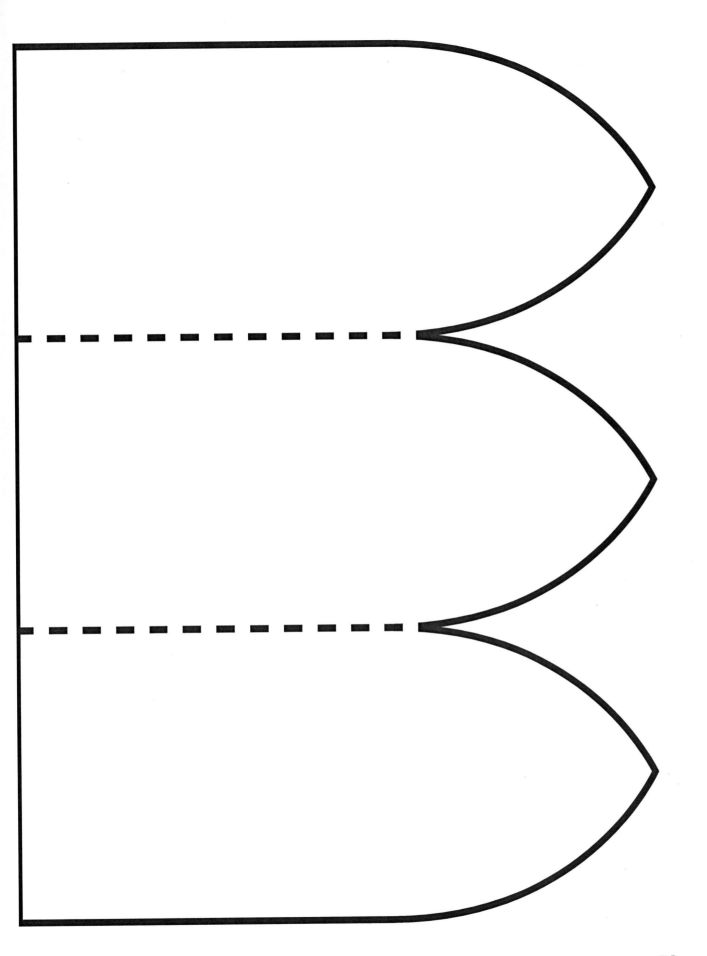

"An Amazing Race" Challenge Stations

Challenge Station 1: The first challenge is the Donkey Station. The children must work together to make a donkey out of a box.

- For each team: place a box (without a lid), a blanket, a stuffed-cloth bundle, crayons, and tape in this station.
- Give each team a box and the photocopy of the donkey's face (below).
- Have the children color the donkey's face and tape it onto the side of the box.
- Have the children pack the blanket and the stuffed-cloth bundle into the box.
- Have the children push the box to the sign that says "Judean Hills."

Challenge Station 2: The second challenge is the Baby Station.

- For each team: place markers and strips of cloth in this station.
- **Say:** Both Mary and Elizabeth were expecting babies. They probably spent time together getting ready for their babies to be born. They would have prepared cloth to swaddle their babies.
- Give the children the strips of cloth. Encourage them to decorate the cloth strips with markers.
- **Say:** The swaddling cloth was wrapped around the baby to keep his or her arms and legs close to the body. The swaddling helped the baby feel safe and secure.
- Have the children pack their swaddling-cloth strips on their donkey, and then push the box donkey to the sign that says "Ein Karem."

The Journey: Walking the Road to Bethlehem Children's Edition

Get ready for your journey to Ein Karem.

Make a box donkey.

Challenge 1

We have used all the water we brought on our journey.

What should we do?

Clue 1

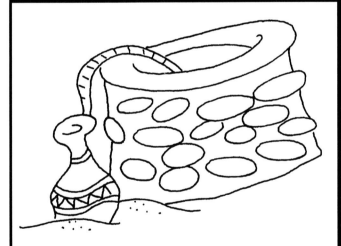

See the vineyards? You're getting close. Just look for a bunch of grapes.

Clue 2

Get ready for the babies.
Make swaddling cloths.

Challenge 2

Nazareth

Judean Hills

Ein Karem

Baby Talk

by Daphna Flegal

(Elizabeth enters holding one of the box rattles made earlier. Elizabeth shakes the rattle every time she says the word baby.*)*

Welcome to my home. *(Elizabeth bows.)* I'm so glad to see you. I've already welcomed one visitor today. Mary is also here. She came all the way from Nazareth to stay with me until my **baby** *(shake rattle)* is born.

My **baby** *(shake rattle)*. Aren't those amazing words? I mean, look at me. You probably think I'm too old to be pregnant, but I'm not. Remember, nothing is impossible with God. My **baby** *(shake rattle)* will be born in about three months, and we're going to name him John. I am so happy.

Mary came to tell me her secret, but even before she told me, I knew. In fact, when I saw her, my **baby** *(shake rattle)* jumped for joy. You see, Mary is also pregnant—and her **baby** *(shake rattle)* is the Son of God. What a blessing!

You know, I think Mary is even happier than I am about our **babies** *(shake rattle)*. As soon as she saw me, she began singing for joy, "My soul magnifies the Lord, and my spirit rejoices in God my Savior." *(Elizabeth sighs.)* Such a beautiful song.

Well, come on in and I'll introduce you to Mary. But I should warn you, with two pregnant women in the house, the only thing we talk about is **babies** *(shake rattle)*.

(Elizabeth exits, shaking the rattle.)

Bible Verse Card

My soul magnifies the Lord,

and my spirit rejoices

in God my Savior.

Luke 1:46-47, NRSV

4 The Journey to Bethlehem

Objectives

The children will
- hear Luke 2:1-7.
- learn that Mary and Joseph traveled to Bethlehem to register for the Roman census.
- discover that Jesus, God's Son, was born in a stable.
- celebrate the birth of Jesus by helping others.

Bible Story

Luke 2:1-7, CEB: Jesus is born in Bethlehem.

Bible Verse

Luke 2:7, CEB: She gave birth to her firstborn son, wrapped him snugly, and laid him in a manger, because there was no place for them in the guestroom.

Focus for the Teacher

The Journey

Mary was nine months pregnant when the Roman Emperor, Caesar Augustus, gave the order for a census. The purpose of the census was to raise tax money. Each man was required to go to the home of his ancestors. Because Joseph was part of the house of David, Mary and Joseph had to travel from Nazareth to Bethlehem. Caesar Augustus did not care that it was a ten-day journey or that Mary was about to have a baby.

Travelers depended on the hospitality of the townspeople. Strangers could expect to be welcomed in people's homes as they traveled, and for the time that the travelers stayed, they were considered part of the family. Because of the crowded conditions in Bethlehem, Mary and Joseph were unable to find a place to stay, either in a private home or in a guesthouse or inn. Some scholars suggest that the real reason Mary and Joseph were not given a guest room is because giving birth in the house would have made the house ritually unclean. Whatever the reason, God's Son was born in a stable.

> She gave birth to her firstborn son, wrapped him snugly, and laid him in a manger, because there was no place for them in the guestroom.
>
> Luke 2:7, CEB

The Bible Verse

When the time came for Mary to give birth, she did all the things a New Testament mother would have done. She washed her baby's body and rubbed him with salt. This custom was meant to firm and tighten the baby's skin. Then she wrapped him in bands of soft cloth. These bands kept the baby warm and helped his body grow straight and strong. Then Mary laid baby Jesus in a manger, a feeding trough for animals.

Which Way to Bethlehem?

There are two possible routes Mary and Joseph traveled from Nazareth to Bethlehem. The more common belief is that the took the route which avoided Samaria. Remember, Jews and Samaritans did not get along. This route would have taken them twenty or thirty miles out of their way into the Jordan Valley and through the Judean desert. The second possible route was along the way known as "The Road of the Patriarchs." This route was often used by pilgrims going to Jerusalem for the Passover.

Explore Interest Groups

Be sure that adult leaders are waiting when the first child arrives. Greet and welcome each child. Get the child involved in an activity that interests him or her and introduces the theme for the day's activities.

By Order of Caesar Augustus

- Help the children experience Mary and Joseph's journey to Bethlehem. Set up a Nazareth station. You may want to decorate the station to look like a Bible-times home. Place the trail-mix ingredients in this station.

- Recruit an adult or teenager to dress as a Roman soldier and greet each child at the door. The Roman soldier will also take part in the "Count Me Out" activity on page 49.

- **Soldier says:** By order of Caesar Augustus, you must be registered as part of the census. Because you are part of the family of King David, you must go from Nazareth to Bethlehem.

- Have the children start at Nazareth.

- Give each child a resealable plastic bag. Use a permanent marker to write each child's name on her or his bag.

- **Say:** You will need to pack food for your journey to Bethlehem. Choose what you want to eat and place it in this bag. It will take you ten days to make the trip, so be sure to pack enough food.

- Let the children choose from the foods you have provided. Use a measuring cup to scoop their choices into their bags. Help the children seal their bags shut.

- **Say:** Now you are ready for the journey.

The Journey—Day 1

- Use masking tape to make a hopscotch game similar to the sample at right that is large enough for two students to play at a time. If you have a large number of children, make more than one hopscotch grid.

- Have each child choose a partner.

- **Say:** Link arms with your partner. Hold your food bag in your other hand. Each of you must hop together to each numbered space, but you can only hop on one foot. When you get to spaces 4, 5, 6, and 7, one partner hops on 4 and 5 and the other partner hops on 6 and 7. The object is to get all the way to Bethlehem without putting both feet down.

- Encourage each set of partners to hop the journey from Nazareth to Bethlehem.

- As each set finishes, let them sit down for a few minutes to rest and eat part of their trail mix.

Prepare

- ✓ Provide raisins, dried apricots, different kinds of oat or wheat cereal, resealable plastic bags, permanent marker, measuring cups, and containers.

- ✓ Photocopy the "Nazareth" sign from Lesson 3 (page 42). Display the sign in the Nazareth station.

- ✓ Place each food item in a different container. Have a measuring cup for each container.

- ✓ Recruit an adult or teenager to portray a Roman soldier. Provide a costume.

Prepare

- ✓ Provide masking tape.

- ✓ Use the masking tape to make a hopscotch game.

| 10 Bethlehem |
| 9 Water |
| 8 Food |
| 5 Feed Donkey / 7 Rest / 6 Water / 4 Food |
| 3 Water |
| 2 Food |
| 1 Start |

- **Say:** You have traveled one day on your journey from Nazareth to Bethlehem. Now you can stop and rest, and have your evening meal.

The Journey—Days 2–10

- Have the children leave their food bags in an out-of-the-way spot. This will be the desert.

- Select one child to be Joseph. Have the remaining children bring chairs to an open area of the room. Instruct the children to arrange the chairs in a line, side by side. Then turn every other chair in the opposite direction. There should be one less chair than the number of children present. If you have a large number of children, you may want to make more than one set of chairs.

- **Say:** Mary and Joseph traveled for ten days to get to Bethlehem. Part of their journey was probably through a desert. We have already traveled one day. Let's pretend to travel nine more days. Joseph will lead us on a journey around the chairs. While you are traveling, I will play some music. When the music stops, it means you have traveled one whole day and it is time to stop and rest. Everyone, including Joseph, must try to find a chair. Whoever winds up without a chair is lost in the desert. But don't be sad! While you are wandering in the desert, you may get your food bag and enjoy your snack.

- Play the music and have Joseph lead the children around the chairs. Stop the music and let the children scramble for the chairs. The child who is left is out of the game goes to the desert. Remove a chair and continue playing the game for eight more rounds.

- **Say:** Finally, we have arrived at Bethlehem!

The Census

- **Say:** We'd better stop and register for the census before we do anything else.

- Have the children move to the census table. Give each child a copy of the census form (page 52, bottom).

- Assign each child a number. Have the child write the number in the box provided (at top right).

- Show each child how to press a thumb onto a nonpermanent ink pad or paint pad and then make a thumbprint in the space provided. Instruct the children to wash their hands after making the thumbprints.

- Have each child write his or her name in the space provided.

- Collect the census forms to use at the end of large-group time.

Prepare

✓ Provide chairs, CD player, and a CD of praise music.

Prepare

✓ Provide a small table or large box, crayons or markers, nonpermanent ink pad or paint pad, paper towels, shallow tray, washable paint, and hand-washing supplies.

✓ Photocopy the sign, "Bethlehem Census" (page 52, top). Photocopy the census form (page 52, bottom) for each child.

✓ Make a census booth out of a small table or large box. Display the "Bethlehem Census" sign on the table.

The Inn

- **Say:** I'm so tired. It's been a long, long journey, but it's finally over. I hope we can find a place to stay.

- Lead the children around the room. End the walk at your art or activity table. Have the children sit down.

- **Say:** The inn in Bethlehem was probably just a guest room or guesthouse. The Bible tells us that this guest room was already taken, so Mary and Joseph were allowed to stay in the stable. The stable might have been in the lower level of the house or even in a cave.

Great Artists at Work

- **Say:** That night in Bethlehem, baby Jesus was born. Mary wrapped baby Jesus in soft cloths and put him to bed in a manger. A manger is a feed box for animals. I wonder what it looked like in the stable.

- **Ask:** What animals do you think were in the stable? Do you think they came close to their feed box to see the baby?

- **Say:** Many great artists have painted pictures of the Nativity during the two thousand years since Jesus was born. Today we are going to look at a more modern artist, Marc Chagall. Chagall was born in Russia in the late 1800s. He was Jewish, but he painted biblical scenes from both the Old and New Testaments.

- Show the children *Nativity* by Marc Chagall.

- **Say:** Marc Chagall painted this picture in 1950. When he painted, he often used bright colors and a painting style called *surrealism*. Surrealism is dreamlike—some parts of the painting might be upside down or some parts might be bigger than you expect them to be, like the cow in this painting. Let's make a surrealist painting of Jesus' birth.

- Give each child a piece of paper. Have them draw Mary and baby Jesus on one side of the paper and Joseph on the opposite side of the paper. Then encourage them to decide what animal will be in the center of their paintings, like Marc Chagall's cow.

- **Say:** You can choose any animal you want to draw in the middle, and you can make the animal any color you want. Remember, it is supposed to be dreamlike. In fact, you can even draw your animal floating in the air or upside down.

- When the children have finished their drawings, have them trace over all their lines with crayons of different colors. Encourage them to make heavy marks.

- Have the children wear smocks. Place the watercolor paints and containers of water on the table. Let the children paint over their entire drawings with watercolor.

- Set the paintings aside to dry. Save the paintings for the art show in Lesson 5.

Prepare

- ✓ Provide drawing paper, pencils, crayons, watercolor paints, paintbrushes, containers of water, recycled newspaper or plastic tablecloth and smocks.

- ✓ Cover the table with newspapers or a plastic tablecloth.

- ✓ Provide a copy of *Nativity* by Marc Chagall. Search the library for images or online at: *http://rubinart.com/Print-Marc-Chagall-907*

NOTE: Websites are constantly changing. Although these websites were checked at the time this book was edited, we recommend that you double-check the site to verify that it is still live and that it is still appropriate for children before doing the activity.

Large Group

Bring all the children together to experience the Bible story. Use jingle bells to alert the children to the large-group time.

No Vacancies

- **Say:** When Mary and Joseph arrived in Bethlehem, there was no room at the inn. The inn was probably a guest room. There is a sign for a guest room in each corner of our room—Guest Room 1, Guest Room 2, Guest Room 3, and Guest Room 4. And there is a sign for each guest room inside this bag. There is also a sign for the stable on the floor in the middle of the room. When you hear music, move around the room. When the music stops, go to one of the guest rooms. I'll pick someone to pull a sign out of this bag. If I pull out the guest-room number from your corner, it means there is no room and you must go to the stable.

- Stop the music and let the children move to one of the four corners.

- Choose a child to select one of the signs from the bag.

- The children standing in the matching corner are out of the game and must sit down in the stable area.

- Start the music again and have the children move around the room. Continue the game until everyone is sitting "in the stable."

Now Appearing at the Stable

- Have the children stay seated in the stable area.

- **Say:** Today we will present the Bible story in a type of drama called Readers' Theater. The actors will read their parts without moving around the stage area. The drama takes place inside the stable in Bethlehem, just before Mary and Joseph arrive. I wonder how the animals might have felt that night to have their space invaded.

- Have the actors line up across the stage area. You may want to use music stands to hold each actor's script.

- Let the actors present "The Not-So-Silent Night" to the children.

In the Stable

- Have the children sit in a circle on the floor. If you have a large group of children, you may want to have more than one circle.

- **Say:** Let's play a game as we think about the place where baby Jesus was born. I will choose one of you to be IT. IT will sit in the center of the circle blindfolded. I will choose people to come up and make the sound of an animal that might be found in a Bible-times stable. Let's see if IT can guess who is making the sound.

Prepare

✓ Provide a CD of Christmas music, CD player, tape, scissors, and a paper bag.

✓ Photocopy and cut apart the signs (pages 53-54). You will need two copies of the guest-room signs (page 53).

✓ Tape one guest-room sign in each corner of the room. Place one copy of each guest-room sign inside a paper bag.

✓ Tape the stable sign on the floor in the middle of the room.

Prepare

✓ Recruit five children, youth, or adults to read the drama. Remember that one actor will need to make the sound of a baby crying in addition to reading her or his part.

✓ Photocopy the script (page 55) for the actors.

✓ Optional: provide music stands and simple animal costumes.

Prepare

✓ Provide a blindfold or sleep mask.

- Have IT sit in the center of the circle. Help IT put on the blindfold.

- Point to a child from the circle. Have that child make an animal sound. Give IT three opportunities to guess who is making the sound. If IT guesses correctly, then that person becomes the next IT. If IT guesses incorrectly, then choose another person to make an animal sound.

Bible Verse

- Have the children stay seated in the circle.

- Hold open the Bible and read verse for the children: "She gave birth to her firstborn son, wrapped him snugly, and laid him in a manger, because there was no place for them in the guestroom" (Luke 2:7, CEB).

- **Say:** Listen carefully as I say the Bible verse again. If I say the verse with the word *manger*, then everyone jumps up and changes places in the circle. If I say a different word besides *manger*, everyone stays seated. Let's practice.

- **Say:** She gave birth to her firstborn son, wrapped him snugly, and laid him in a *bathtub…*

- The children stay seated.

- **Say:** She gave birth to her firstborn son, wrapped him snugly, and laid him in a *manger…*

- The children switch places. After they have switched places, encourage everyone to say the Bible verse together.

- Play the game several times, periodically changing the word for manger *(swimming pool, birdbath, football stadium, bunk bed, and so forth)*.

- Be sure to say the Bible verse with the children after saying the verse correctly and having the children switch places.

Prepare
✓ Provide a CEB Bible.

Count Me Out

- Give the children their census forms. Make sure each child knows his or her number on the form.

- **Say:** Mary and Joseph went to Bethlehem because of the Roman census. Each of you was given a census number. When the Roman soldier calls out your number, stand up. The Roman soldier will tell you how to move to your small group.

- Have the Roman soldier call out each child's number. Then have the soldier tell the child how to move *(hop, skip, tiptoe, walk backwards, walk like a camel, march, gallop, jump, take giant steps, take baby steps, and so forth)*.

- Encourage each child to move as told to her or his small group.

- Place the census forms in their map folders.

Prepare
✓ Provide census forms made earlier (page 46).

Small Groups

Divide the children into small groups. You may organize the groups around age levels or around readers and nonreaders. Keep the groups small, with a maximum of ten children in each group. You may need to have more than one of each group.

Young Children

- Give each child the baby Jesus circle you cut out before class. Encourage the children to decorate the circles with crayons or markers.

- **Say:** Our Bible story was about Mary and Joseph's journey to Bethlehem.

- Give each child his or her map-of-Palestine folder. Help the children circle the name *Bethlehem* on their maps using a different color from when they circled Bethlehem in Lesson 2.

- **Ask:** Why did Mary and Joseph go to Bethlehem? *(to be counted as part of the Roman census)*

- Encourage the children to glue the baby Jesus circles somewhere on the edge of the maps.

- Help each child draw a line from the circle to Bethlehem.

- **Ask:** How do you think Mary and Joseph felt when they could not find any place to stay? *(tired and sad)* How do you think Mary and Joseph felt when they were offered the stable? *(relieved, grateful)* What happened in the stable? *(Baby Jesus was born.)*

- Hold open the CEB Bible to Luke 2. Say the verse with the children, "She gave birth to her firstborn son, wrapped him snugly, and laid him in a manger, because there was no place for them in the guestroom."

- **Say:** Our Bible verse tells us that when baby Jesus was born, Mary wrapped him snugly in soft cloths. Mary would have placed baby Jesus on a square of cloth. Then she would have folded the corners over her baby's sides and feet, and wrapped bandages around the whole bundle to keep the baby's arms straight by his sides to help him feel safe and warm. Today we wrap babies in blankets to make them feel safe and warm.

- Give each child a copy of the "Art Show" invitation (page 4).

- **Say:** These are invitations for an art show that we will have during our next lesson. We will display the wonderful art you have made in the last four lessons for your friends and family to enjoy. We will also collect baby blankets to give to mothers who do not have enough money to buy the things they need for their babies. You can bring the blankets as your tickets into the art show.

- Let the children decorate the back of the invitations by gluing on strips of gauze or cloth.

- **Pray:** Thank you, God, for stories from the Bible that tell us about Jesus' birth. We praise you for gift of Jesus. Amen.

Prepare

- ✓ Photocopy the map circles (page 16) and the map of Palestine (page 17) for any child absent for Lessons 1–3.

- ✓ Photocopy the "Art Show" invitation (page 4) for each child.

- ✓ Provide a CEB Bible, the map folders from Lesson 1 (page 12), safety scissors, crayons or markers, glue or gluesticks, and scraps of cloth or strips of gauze.

- ✓ Cut out a map circle of baby Jesus (page 16) for each child.

Older Children

- Give the children the baby Jesus circles. Have the children cut out the circles.

- Encourage the children to decorate the circles with colored pencils.

- **Say:** Today our Bible story was about Mary and Joseph's trip to Bethlehem.

- Give each child her or his map-of-Palestine folder. Help the children circle the name *Bethlehem* on their maps using a different color from when they circled Bethlehem in Lesson 2.

- **Ask:** Why did Mary and Joseph go to Bethlehem? *(to be counted as part of the Roman census)*

- Encourage the children to glue the baby Jesus circles somewhere on the edge of the maps.

- Give each child a length of yarn. Have the child glue the yarn from the circle to Bethlehem.

- **Ask:** How do you think Mary and Joseph felt when they could not find any place to stay? *(tired and sad)* How do you think Mary and Joseph felt when they were offered the stable? *(relieved, grateful)* What happened while Mary and Joseph were in the stable? *(Baby Jesus was born.)*

- Hold open the CEB Bible to Luke 2. Say the verse with the children, "She gave birth to her firstborn son, wrapped him snugly, and laid him in a manger, because there was no place for them in the guestroom."

- **Say:** Our Bible verse tells us that when baby Jesus was born, Mary wrapped him snugly in soft cloths. Mary would have placed baby Jesus on a square of cloth. Then she would have folded the corners over her baby's sides and feet, and wrapped bandages around the whole bundle to keep the baby's arms straight by his sides to help him feel safe and warm. Today we wrap babies in blankets to make them feel safe and warm.

- Give each child a copy of the "Art Show" invitation (page 4).

- **Say:** These are invitations for an art show that we will have during our next lesson. We will display the wonderful art you have made in the last four lessons for your friends and family to enjoy. We will also collect baby blankets to give to mothers who do not have enough money to buy the things they need for their babies. You can bring the blankets as your tickets into the art show.

- Let the children decorate the back of the invitations by gluing on strips of gauze or cloth.

- **Pray:** Thank you, God, for stories from the Bible that tell us about Jesus' birth. We praise you for gift of Jesus. Amen.

Prepare

✓ Photocopy the map circles (page 16) and the map of Palestine (page 17) for any child absent for Lessons 1–3.

✓ Photocopy the "Art Show" invitation (page 4) for each child.

✓ Provide a CEB Bible, the map folders from Lesson 1 (page 12), safety scissors, colored pencils, construction paper, glue or gluesticks, yarn, and scraps of cloth or strips of gauze.

Bethlehem Census

House of David

Register Here

Census

Name _____

Hometown _____

Number of Family Members _____

By order of Caesar Augustus

Number

Thumbprint

The Journey: Walking the Road to Bethlehem Children's Edition

Guest Room 1

Guest Room 2

Guest Room 3

Guest Room 4

Stable

The Journey: Walking the Road to Bethlehem Children's Edition

The Not-So-Silent Night

by LeeDell Stickler

Grumpy Cow: It's past dinnertime. Where's my innkeeper with our hay?

Owl: Whoo?

Sheep: *Our* innkeeper. He's probably busy. There's a lot of people here today.

Dove: Speaking of people, why are two people coming into our stable?

Owl: Whoo?

Grumpy Cow: What? Two people in *my* stable. Just what we need.

Sheep: Get over it, Grumpy. Two people won't take up much space in *our* stable.

Owl: Whoo?

Dove: That man and woman over there.

Owl: Whoo?

Donkey: Sorry to bother you like this. I brought these people here to Bethlehem. But there were no more rooms. Your innkeeper said they could sleep in the stable.

Owl: Whoo?

Grumpy Cow: Oh, just be quiet!

(Everything is quiet. All the animals start snoring. Then, the sound of a baby crying.)

Grumpy Cow: Now, what?

Sheep: It's a baby, silly.

Grumpy Cow: I know it's a baby. But what's it doing here? In *my* stable.

Sheep: In *our* stable!

Donkey: I told you, there were no rooms available.

Sheep: Where's it going to sleep?

Owl: Whoo?

Sheep: The baby.

Donkey: How about that wooden bucket over there. It's nice and strong. It will hold a baby.

Sheep: It's strong, but not very soft. How about that straw basket over there?

Donkey: It's soft, but it's not big enough.

Dove: How about the wooden crate where we doves sleep? It's big and strong.

Donkey: It's big enough. It's strong enough. But it's not very soft.

Grumpy Cow: I've got an idea. They can put the baby in my feed box. It's big enough for a baby. It's strong enough to protect it. And it's soft enough.

Sheep: *Our* feed box!

Grumpy Cow: Whatever. Now, everyone, let's get quiet so the baby can sleep.

Owl: Whoo?

All Animals: Ssssh.

5 The Shepherds

Objectives

The children will
- hear Luke 2:8-20.
- learn that the shepherds were the first to hear the news that Jesus was born.
- discover that the shepherds responded to the angels by immediately going to find Jesus.
- have opportunities to tell about Jesus' birth.

Bible Story

Luke 2:8-20, CEB: Angels tell the shepherds that Jesus is born.

Bible Verse

Luke 2:11, CEB: Your savior is born today in David's city. He is Christ the Lord.

Focus for the Teacher

The Shepherds

Luke tells us that the first to hear the good news of Jesus' birth were shepherds. God chose to proclaim the birth of God's Son not to kings and emperors, but rather to people in the most lowly of positions. God's greatest gift is for all people, regardless of their position in life. God's call comes to everyone.

Shepherds had a hard life. Their work was often dirty, and they were considered unclean. This meant that they could not participate in many of the religious ceremonies. It also meant that the religious leaders looked down on the shepherds. Yet, God chose these people to be the first to know: Your Savior is born!

When the shepherds heard the angel's message, they responded at once. They went immediately to find the baby. And then when they saw the baby, they praised God and told everyone they met the good news that Jesus was born.

The Angels

The Bible does not name the angel who appeared to the shepherds. Nor does the Bible describe what the angel looked like. We do know that the angel was a messenger from God.

> Your savior is born today in David's city. He is Christ the Lord.
>
> Luke 2:11, CEB

The Bible Verse

The angel's message to the shepherds was both significant and surprising. The birth of God's Son was announced to people who had no great status or wealth, people who were even considered outcasts. It is also significant that part of the angel's message is "*your* savior." Jesus was born for each one of us. Our Savior is a personal Savior.

The Common English Bible (CEB) uses the Greek translation for the term *messiah*, which means the "anointed one." It is a title we use for Jesus that points to him as our Savior.

On the Hillside

The fields around Bethlehem did not grow lush with grass. In order for their sheep to graze, shepherds moved them about during the day. At night, the shepherds drove the sheep to a common place for protection. Sometimes the sheep were kept in a sheepfold. This was either an enclosure built with a wall of rocks or a shelter built into a cave. One shepherd would lie down across the opening so that the sheep would not wander out during the night.

Explore Interest Groups

Be sure that adult leaders are waiting when the first child arrives. Greet and welcome each child. Get the child involved in an activity that interests him or her and introduces the theme for the day's activities.

A Good Shepherd

- Recruit an adult or teenager to dress as a shepherd and another adult or teenager to dress as a lamb. Have the shepherd and lamb greet each child at the door. The lamb should only say, "Baa." Have the shepherd and lamb tell today's Bible story in large-group time.

- **The shepherd says:** Welcome! I'm glad you're here to complete the shepherds' training course. First, you will be given your official shepherd's headband. Please begin at the weaver's shop.

- Instruct the child to move to the table with the headband materials.

- Give each child a 6-by-36 cloth strip. Encourage the child to decorate the strip with fabric crayons or permanent markers. If you choose to use permanent markers, have the children wear smocks.

- Help each child tie the strip around her or his head.

- **Say:** Today we are going to be shepherds. Shepherds played an important role in the story of Jesus' birth. In order to be good shepherds, we have to look like shepherds, so wear your headbands proudly.

- Encourage the children to wear their headbands throughout the lesson.

Prepare

✓ Recruit adults or teenagers to portray a shepherd and a lamb.

✓ Provide simple costumes.

✓ Provide strips of cloth (a 6-by-36 strip for each child), a table, and fabric crayons or permanent markers and smocks.

Protect the Flock

- **Say:** Shepherds are important to today's Bible story. The main job of a shepherd in Bible times was to care for and protect the sheep. This was an important job because sheep provided milk, food, and wool for clothes. A shepherd often carried a staff. If sheep fell down when they were heavy with wool, they couldn't get back up on their own. The shepherd used the curved part of the staff to catch hold of sheep that might have fallen or wandered off.

- Let the children work together to make Shepherd's Staff Cookies. Have the children wash their hands.

- Mix together cream cheese, margarine, brown sugar, salt, and vanilla. Blend well. Add flour. Mix together until dough forms a ball.

- Let the children take turns kneading the dough on a floured surface. Add more flour if dough is sticky.

- Give each child some dough and a piece of wax paper. Show each child how to roll the dough on the wax paper into a ropelike shape.

Prepare

✓ Provide cookie ingredients, wax paper, mixing bowl, mixing spoon, measuring cups and spoons, cookie sheets, and hand-washing supplies.

Shepherd's Staff Cookies
3-oz-pkg. soft cream cheese
½ cup soft margarine
½ cup firmly packed brown sugar
½ tsp salt
½ tsp vanilla
1¾ cups flour

- Place the dough on an ungreased cookie sheet. Encourage the child to curve one end into a shepherd's crook.

- Have an adult helper bake the cookies at 350 degrees for eight to ten minutes. Plan to eat the cookies during the art show.

Quiet the Sheep

- **Say:** Shepherds are important to today's Bible story. Sometimes a shepherd played a flute to quiet and soothe the sheep. Flutes in Bible times were often made out of reeds tied together with cord.

- Encourage the children to make a double flute out of drinking straws.

- Give each child two drinking straws. Show the child how to cut one straw one half inch shorter than the second straw. Precut the straws for younger children.

- Give each child some plastic clay. Instruct each child to tear off two small pieces of the clay and roll the pieces into pea-sized balls.

- Have the children plug one end of each straw with the balls of plastic clay. It is better to plug the cut ends of the straws.

- Have each child hold the two straws side by side, with the open end of the straws lined up evenly. Help each child wrap a piece of tape around the two straws to hold them together.

- Show the children how to hold the flutes vertically, then blow across the open ends. Listen to the sounds.

Prepare

✓ Provide two plastic drinking straws for each child, safety scissors, tape, rulers, and plastic clay.

✓ Precut the straws for younger children.

Touch the Sheep

- Make a display of unwashed wool (or wool fabric) and scraps of wool yarn. Invite the children to touch and handle all of the wool.

- **Say:** Sheep were very important in Bible times. The wool from the sheep was spun into yarn, and the yarn was woven into cloth. Sheep were also a source of milk, cheese, and meat.

- Let the children use scraps of wool yarn to make Christmas cards.

- Give each child a piece of construction paper. Show the children how to fold the paper in half to make a card.

- Have the children open the card to the inside. Help the children write "Your Savior is born!" inside the card. You may need to write the words for younger children.

- Have the children close their cards so the cover is facing up.

- Encourage the children to decorate the covers with scraps of yarn.

- **Say:** Our Bible story begins with shepherds in the fields around Bethlehem, watching over their sheep.

- Set the cards aside to dry. Plan to use the cards in small-group time.

Prepare

✓ Provide unwashed wool or wool fabric, wool yarn, construction paper, markers, glue, and safety scissors.

✓ Cut the yarn into small pieces.

Be the First to See Jesus!

- Divide the children into teams. Have the teams move to one side of the room.

- Use tape to mark a starting line and a finish line.

- Place a Nativity set just past the finish line.

- **Say:** We have been learning about shepherds and that they are important to today's Bible story. The shepherds are important because they were the first to hear about Jesus' birth. While they were on the hillside near Bethlehem, an angel appeared to them and told them that Jesus was born. When the shepherds heard the news, they hurried to Bethlehem to see the baby.

- Begin with the first team. Have them line up along the starting line.

- **Say:** Shepherds on Team One, I want you to hop to Bethlehem.

- Have the children in Team One hop to the finish line. The first person crossing the finish line is the winner.

- Continue with each team. Change how you tell each team to move. *(tiptoe, march, take giant steps, take baby steps, gallop, walk backwards)*

- When all the teams have had a turn, let the winners from each team make up a final team.

Prepare

✓ Provide masking tape and a Nativity set.

Art Show

- Have the children help you set up for the art show.

- **Say:** Many artists have made pictures that tell different parts of the story of what happened when Jesus was born. You are some of those artists! Today we are having an art show to share your artwork with your family and friends.

- Let the children place their artwork around the room. You might mount them on a bulletin board or wall, on a folding screen, or place them on tables.

- Make a refreshment table. Cover a table with a plastic or paper tablecloth, and place napkins on the table. Set out the Shepherd's Staff Cookies made earlier (page 57). If desired, serve punch or water.

- Encourage your children to welcome your visitors as they arrive.

- Accept any baby blankets your visitors may have brought, and set them aside to deliver to whatever ministry you have chosen to receive the gifts.

- Have the children show the artwork to the visitors. Encourage the children to tell the Bible story that goes with the art.

- Invite the visitors to stay for large-group time.

Prepare

✓ Provide tape or plastic clay to mount artwork.

✓ Provide artwork the children made in previous lessons.

✓ Provide a plastic or paper tablecloth, napkins, and the Shepherd's Staff Cookies made earlier (page 57).

✓ Optional: provide punch or water and cups.

Large Group

Bring all the children together to experience the Bible story. Use jingle bells to alert the children to the large-group time.

Call the Sheep

- Have the children move to an open area of the room. Invite your visitors to play the game with the children.

- Choose one child to be the shepherd. The remaining children are sheep.

- **Say:** Shepherds are important to today's Bible story. Every shepherd knew his sheep. The sheep knew the sound of the shepherd's voice. Each of you is a sheep. Some of you will belong to our shepherd. Some will not. Our shepherd must find the sheep that belongs to her or him.

- Have your shepherd close his or her eyes or leave the room with another adult.

- Choose two or three children to be the sheep belonging to your shepherd. Have your shepherd open her or his eyes or come back to the room.

- Have your shepherd call out, "Here, sheep." All the sheep hold their hands up over their mouths. But only the chosen sheep answer, "Baa, baa." The shepherd must find the sheep that belong to him or her.

- When the shepherd has found all the sheep, have the sheep sit down in your large-group area.

- Choose new shepherds and sheep. Play until everyone is sitting.

Now Appearing on the Hillside

- Have the children stay seated in the stable area.

- **Say:** We have a special visitor today. He is a shepherd, and he brought one of his sheep with him.

- Have the shepherd tell the story, "A Savior in a Manger," to the children. The lamb's only response is "Baaa!" But each time the lamb responds, it should be with the emotion that would be appropriate to the story that is being told.

Story Charades

- Divide your children into at least two teams. Invite your visitors to play charades with the children.

- **Say:** We have been learning about the different people who were part of the story of Jesus' birth. Let's play a game of charades to review what happened.

- Have each team move to a different area of the room.

Prepare

- ✓ Recruit a youth or adult to portray the shepherd, and another youth or adult to portray the lamb.

- ✓ Photocopy the script (page 64) for the actors.

- ✓ Provide simple costumes.

- Tell each team the scenes they are to portray: Mary and Gabriel; Joseph and the angel; Mary and Elizabeth; Mary and Joseph and the donkey; Mary and Joseph and baby Jesus in the stable; the shepherds and the angels; the shepherds at the manger. Mix up the scenes so that they are not in story order.

- Give each team a few moments to decide on how they will act out the scene.

- Have the first team act out the scene with no talking. The other team has one minute to guess the scene.

- After guessing the scene ask the children if they can remember where the scene took place. *(Mary and Gabriel—Nazareth; Joseph and the angel— Bethlehem; Mary and Elizabeth—Ein Karem; Mary and Joseph and the donkey—Bethlehem; Mary and Joseph and baby Jesus in the stable— Bethlehem; the shepherds and the angels—Bethlehem; the shepherds at the manger—Bethlehem)*

- Then let the next team act out their scene, and have the first team do the guessing.

- Continue alternating teams until you have acted out all of the scenes and remembered where the scenes took place.

Bible Verse

- Have the children stay seated in the circle.

- Hold open the Bible and read verse for the children: "Your savior is born today in David's city. He is Christ the Lord" (Luke 2:11, CEB).

- Teach the children and visitors the American Sign Language signs for the words *Christ* and *Lord*.

Prepare
✓ Provide a CEB Bible.

Christ— Make a "C" with the right hand. Place "C" at the left shoulder and then move across the body to the right waist.

Lord—Make an "L" with the right hand. Place "L" at the left shoulder and then move across the body to the right waist.

- **Say:** Listen as I say the first part of the verse, "Your savior is born today in David's city." Then you stand up, sign, and say, "He is Christ the Lord."

- Say the first part of the verse several times and encourage the children and visitors to respond with rest of the verse.

- Thank your visitors for coming. Send the children to their small groups.

Small Groups

Divide the children into small groups. You may organize the groups around age levels or around readers and nonreaders. Keep the groups small, with a maximum of ten children in each group. You may need to have more than one of each group.

Young Children

- Give each child the shepherds circle you cut out before class. Encourage the children to decorate the circles with crayons or markers.

- **Say:** Our Bible story was about the shepherds who were watching their sheep on the hillside in Bethlehem.

- Give each child his or her map-of-Palestine folder. Help the children circle the name *Bethlehem* on their maps using a different color from when they circled Bethlehem in Lessons 2 and 4.

- **Ask:** What were the shepherds doing on the hillside during the night Jesus was born? *(watching and protecting their sheep)*

- Encourage the children to glue the shepherds circles somewhere on the edge of the maps.

- Help each child draw a line from the circle to Bethlehem.

- **Ask:** How do you think the shepherds felt when they saw the angel? *(afraid, surprised)* How do you think the shepherds felt when they heard the angel's message? *(amazed, joyful)* What did the shepherds do after they saw the angels? *(hurry to see baby Jesus)*

- Hold open the CEB Bible to Luke 2:11. Say the verse with the children, "Your savior is born today in David's city. He is Christ the Lord."

- **Say:** Our Bible verse tells us that the shepherds hurried to Bethlehem to see the baby. After they found baby Jesus, they praised God and told everyone about baby Jesus.

- **Ask:** What are some ways you can tell your family and friends about Jesus' birth? *(send Christmas cards, text, call on the telephone, e-mail)*

- Give each child a glass jar to decorate like stained glass.

- Give the children scraps of colored tissue paper. Let the children tear the tissue paper into smaller pieces.

- Have the children glue the tissue paper all around the glass jar. When the children have finished gluing on the tissue paper, show them how to brush watered-down glue over the entire outside of the jar.

- Give the children the copies of the good-news messages. Encourage each child to put the four messages inside her or his jar. Let the jars dry.

- **Say:** Place your jar in your home. Invite members of your family to take out a message and read it each time they pass by the jar.

- **Pray:** Thank you, God, for Jesus, our Savior. Amen.

Prepare

✓ Photocopy the map circles (page 16) and the map of Palestine (page 17) for any child absent for Lessons 1–4.

✓ Provide CEB Bibles, pencils, crayons or markers, colored tissue paper, scissors, glue, glue brushes, water, plastic containers, and a small glass jar for each child.

✓ Photocopy and cut apart the four good-news messages (page 64, bottom) for each child.

✓ Cut out a map circle of the shepherds for each child (page 16).

✓ Pour glue into plastic containers. Add a small amount of water.

Older Children

- Give the children the shepherds circles. Have the children cut out the circles.

- Encourage the children to decorate the circles with colored pencils.

- **Say:** Our Bible story was about the shepherds who were watching their sheep on the hillside in Bethlehem.

- Give each child his or her map-of-Palestine folder. Help the children circle the name *Bethlehem* on their maps using a different color from when they circled Bethlehem in Lessons 2 and 4.

- **Ask:** What were the shepherds doing on the hillside during the night Jesus was born? *(watching and protecting their sheep)*

- Encourage the children to glue the shepherds circles somewhere on the edge of the maps.

- Give each child a length of yarn. Have the child glue the yarn from the circle to Bethlehem.

- **Ask:** How do you think the shepherds felt when they saw the angel? *(afraid, surprised)* How do you think the shepherds felt when they heard the angel's message? *(amazed, joyful)* What did the shepherds do after they saw the angels? *(hurry to see baby Jesus)*

- Hold open the CEB Bible to Luke 2:11. Say the verse with the children, "Your savior is born today in David's city. He is Christ the Lord."

- **Say:** Our Bible verse tells us that the shepherds hurried to Bethlehem to see the baby. After they found baby Jesus, they praised God and told everyone about baby Jesus.

- **Ask:** What are some ways you can tell your family and friends about Jesus' birth? *(send Christmas cards, text, call on the telephone, e-mail)*

- Give each child a glass jar to decorate like stained glass.

- Give the children scraps of colored tissue paper. Let the children tear the tissue paper into smaller pieces.

- Have the children glue the tissue paper all around the glass jar. When the children have finished gluing on the tissue paper, show them how to brush watered-down glue over the entire outside of the jar.

- Give the children the copies of the four good-news messages (page 64, bottom). Let the children cut the messages apart.

- Encourage each child to put the four messages inside her or his jar. Let the jars dry.

- **Say:** Place your jar in your home. Invite members of your family to take out a message and read it each time they pass by the jar.

- **Pray:** Thank you, God, for Jesus, our Savior. Amen.

Prepare

- ✓ Photocopy the map circles (page 16) and the map of Palestine (page 17) for any child absent for Lessons 1–4.

- ✓ Provide CEB Bibles, yarn, colored pencils, colored tissue paper, scissors, glue, glue brushes, water, plastic containers, and a small glass jar for each child.

- ✓ Photocopy the four good-news messages (page 64, bottom) for each child.

- ✓ Pour glue into plastic containers. Add a small amount of water.

A Savior in a Manger

by Sharilyn S. Adair

Shepherd: It was very late. The sheep were all settled for the night.

Lamb: Baaa!

Shepherd: I was so tired. I had just laid down across the sheepfold gate to keep the sheep in for the night. I stretched out and looked at the stars.

Lamb: Baaa!

Shepherd: The sky began to get lighter. That wasn't right. *(Shake head, "no.")* Soon the sky was so light that it was though it were daylight.

Lamb: Baaa!

Shepherd: I called out to my friends: "Wake up! Wake up! Something is happening!"

Lamb: Baaa!

Shepherd: The light was so bright that I could barely look at it. *(Put arms over face as though shielding it from the bright light.)*

Lamb: Baaa!

Shepherd: We were all frightened. Then we heard a voice say, "Don't be afraid."

Lamb: Baaa!

Shepherd: Don't be afraid? Of course, we were afraid! We were looking at an angel. And the angel was talking to *us.* "I bring good news to you and for all the people. Your Savior is born today in David's city. He is Christ the Lord."

Lamb: Baaa!

Shepherd: Our Savior! Our Savior has come! We have been waiting for years to hear this.

Lamb: Baaa!

Shepherd: How will we know where to find this child? I asked the angel. And the angel said, "You will find a newborn baby wrapped snugly and lying in a manger."

Lamb: Baaa!

Shepherd: Our Savior in a manger? Surely, they were mistaken. A savior should come to a palace.

Lamb: Baaa!

Shepherd: Suddenly, there was not just one angel but many. The sky was filled with their song. "Glory to God in heaven and peace to all people on earth."

Lamb: Baaa!

Shepherd: As quickly as the angels had appeared, they were gone. My friends and I decided we had to see what the angels were talking about. So we set off for Bethlehem to find this baby.

Lamb: Baaa!

Shepherd: When we got to Bethlehem, we searched until we found the stable. When we found it, there were Mary, Joseph, and the baby. And the baby was lying in a manger!

Lamb: Baaa!

Shepherd: We knelt beside the manger. This was the Savior God told us was coming.

Lamb: Baaa!

Shepherd: As we left the city and went back to the hills, we told everyone we saw about the angels, the message, and the baby sleeping in the manger.

"Your savior is born today in David's city. He is Christ the Lord" (Luke 2:11, CEB).	"My soul magnifies the Lord, and my spirit rejoices in God my Savior" (Luke 1:46-47, NRSV).
"She gave birth to her firstborn son, wrapped him snugly, and laid him in a manger, because there was no place for them in the guestroom" (Luke 2:7, CEB).	*"And they will call him,* Emmanuel. (*Emmanuel* means 'God with us.')" (Matthew 1:23, CEB).

The Journey: Walking the Road to Bethlehem Children's Edition

CPSIA information can be obtained at www.ICGtesting.com
Printed in the USA
LVOW021039181111

255595LV00001B/2/P

9 781426 728570